PREVENTING PLAGIARISM

Preventing Plagiarism

Tips and Techniques

LAURA HENNESSEY DESENA

*New York University, School of Continuing
and Professional Studies*
West Milford Public High School, New Jersey

National Council of Teachers of English
1111 W. Kenyon Road, Urbana, Illinois 61801-1096

Staff Editor: Bonny Graham
Manuscript Editor: Jane Curran
Interior Design: Jenny Jensen Greenleaf
Cover Design: Jody A. Boles

NCTE Stock Number: 45937

It is the policy of NCTE in its journals and other publications to provide a forum for the open discussion of ideas concerning the content and the teaching of English and the language arts. Publicity accorded to any particular point of view does not imply endorsement by the Executive Committee, the Board of Directors, or the membership at large, except in announcements of policy, where such endorsement is clearly specified.

Every effort has been made to provide current URLs and email addresses, but because of the rapidly changing nature of the Web, some sites and addresses may no longer be accessible.

Library of Congress Cataloging-in-Publication Data

DeSena, Laura Hennessey, 1961–
    Preventing plagiarism : tips and techniques / Laura Hennessey DeSena.
        p. cm.
    Includes bibliographical references.
    ISBN 978-0-8141-4593-7 ((pbk))
1. Plagiarism—Prevention. 2. Cheating (Education)—Prevention. I. Title.
    PN167.D47 2007
    371.5'8—dc22
                                                    2006036980

To my own original thinkers, Bronwen and Aidan

Contents

ACKNOWLEDGMENTS

I wish to thank my students (at New York University and at West Milford High School in New Jersey), who have had the most profound effect on how I teach writing. And, of course, I want to thank my family for loving and supporting me through the initial freewriting and the final formal writing of this book.

The Rewards of Original Thinking

Writing Is a Dialogue

Writing is not merely a form of communication—a vehicle for the transference of ideas from writer to reader. The act of writing is a study of self: a process that moves inward, the pen like a divining rod; then outward, in the stream of ideas selected to be shared with others.

Research is not simply the acquiring of information: it is the assimilation of information. It requires the researcher to have a voice in the world that first satisfies self. Research combines the process of self-discovery with external discovery—through the lens of point of view, in an examination of information outside of self. Cacophony becomes dialogue. It is the job of the writer of research to modulate the voices of the outsiders through the subjective eye/I.

Research writing is a contribution to academia. It should not be mere regurgitation of the facts and ideas of scholars and specialists. As educators, we must teach students to realize that they are required to have their *own* insights into source materials. They must engage in a dialogue with the sources they consult. Without this dialogue their research is meaningless and becomes a mere exercise of collecting and organizing.

We must make the distinction between reporting and researching. Writing a report is objective writing; writing a research paper is subjective writing. Research is not simply finding information: it is processing information. Researching a topic requires a filtering of sources through a unique point of view. Research is a dynamic cerebral activity; reporting is a mechanical one.

Reporting is a retelling of ideas found; it is not an analysis of ideas found. Although reporting involves the gathering of information, it does not require a response; it does not require engagement. Often, for the student writer, reporting is a mere transcribing of information. And it can be, in this electronic age, a mere cutting and pasting: students may not even read the information they are incorporating into their "reports." More disconcerting than this is what Thomas Mallon reasons in his afterword to the new edition of *Stolen Words:*

> For students, especially, the Internet may sap the very need to create. *It's all there already*, or so it seems; all the knowledge on a given subject, and all the competing viewpoints, in a machine you can carry around like a book. What's there to add—and why dig a well instead of turning on the tap? (246)

The Internet becomes the authority students will not question—perhaps because they do not recognize a need to, but mostly because of lethargy: why exert the effort to track down legitimate scholarly sources and why bother to think at all? Tomes, authoritative texts, always inspire confidence—knowledge in hard copy, something solid and real. But now, with the dissemination of information (not all of it truth/knowledge) over the Internet, as Mallon points out, there is a sense of the paradoxically definitive in the apparently infinite. With hyperlink text there is an impression of the depths of a topic already plumbed. The vastness of the Internet becomes more intimidating to a student writer than the solidity of a book. It was hard enough to challenge the concrete in a print-based world, but how can a student possibly challenge the infinite and abstract world of the Internet?

To teach students how to write an authentic research paper, we have to inspire in them a confidence to find a point of entry—this point of entry is an opening through the primary source(s): Alice should go down the rabbit hole, rather than pass through the looking glass of reflection, one that *represents* the environment for her. The experience must be a journey, if it is to be worthwhile.

All too often teachers emphasize the content (the information) students will cull and hopefully learn. But it is our obligation as teachers to encourage them to respond to the expert or scholar, to answer his or her underlying claim, to affirm it or to deny it. Or, in a more sophisticated paper, embrace the complexities, the subtleties of the text(s) under consideration. Students are so used to receiving information (from television and other electronic sources); they are constantly taking in—we need to teach them how to interpret and respond.

In student research papers, there should be some tangible base grounded in the primary sources. There should be some hypothesizing from primary materials, before secondhand information is read and accepted like a handout to those in desperate need. Secondary source information is better appreciated and better understood when students have worked hard to arrive at understandings of their own, when students have struggled with the firsthand information. Give students some experience of the authentic process, not the rotely conventional one that moves from grabbing up secondary sources into note taking, from there into organizing a mere report—stale because in it information went unchallenged, unprocessed by the student.

I recognize that students are often given assignments to which they cannot relate, topics about which they have no desire to write. They come from a place far away from interest in the topic, and yet the parameters are set for them. We must encourage them to see how they are involved in the subject *through the act of writing alone*. By fully exploring the research materials, by analyzing, by recognizing a topical reaction for what it is, just that, they will be forced to delve more deeply inside themselves to find a way into the subject. Research will reveal their ideas even as the ideas of others are revealed to them. This is the tension that makes the experience authentic. If research moves in one direction only, it is not successful.

If research is productive, researchers are finally confronted with themselves—their innermost thoughts, their belief systems, their moral values, their aesthetic values. Through research students learn content: it is, after all, a journey through unfamiliar territories: the subject matter and the subjective eye. Research is not successful unless students receive knowledge about both.

The Dubious Book Report v. the Authentic Literary Analysis Paper

In requiring students to read, we ask them to demonstrate, to document that they have read. Often we become obsessive about proving to ourselves, as teachers, that all students have completed the reading assignment. We ask for the book report. What is the classic book report? It is pure plot summary, regurgitation that ultimately encourages plagiarism in that it asks for no insights from the students. We place them in this mode early on. Unfortunately, this retelling of the text is useless for several reasons—foremost among them is that it is a shabby mimicking of the original. No one can write Poe's "The Fall of the House of Usher" as well as Poe, nor should another writer attempt to.

I call this the dubious book report. What has been gained by the assignment? Little in the way of engagement, and in this technological age when students can cut and paste information, they may be completely disengaged through use of online study guides. Even if they are working from the literature itself, in a book report, they are retelling the story, reciting it and, therefore, not responding to it. Their papers will be narrative in structure because they are following the author's organization. This means, of course, that they are not shaping an argument—that they are not analyzing the text. In the conventional book report template, the only place for student evaluation of text is in the final paragraph, which is typically a general recommendation of the novel to other students because it is "good." What teachers should encourage, instead, is that students attempt to understand the literature through the process of writing. My recommendation is going to be an emphasis on freewriting as a way to engage in a dialogue with the novel/play/poem.

We must require students to write a critical analysis of the literature, so that they begin to understand subjective writing as a dialogue, in which the crucial conversation is between the student and the primary source(s). If research is required by the teacher (this assignment is usually called the term paper), other voices will be joining this central exchange of ideas.

Writing a subjective paper requires students to pull something out of themselves, to search through their own ideas on a subject. They may dredge up their preconceived notions about a topic and compare them to or contrast them with credible sources of information; they may find they disagree with a literary critic's interpretation of a primary source because they did not fully comprehend the text, and so they have been forced to study it again; they may have fully comprehended the primary source and find that the critic has taken too great an interpretive risk with the evidence. All of these are positive results of responding to the information. The student will be challenged because he or she is required to have a voice in the midst of these heavyweights—the experts and scholars. How can what students have to say about a primary source be valid? We must teach them to be meticulous readers but also teach them to craft arguments, to ground their understandings in the evidence (primary, as well as secondary source evidence).

Obviously, we understand that various critical positions can exist in the world; they are not mutually exclusive: this is critical discourse. Students often do not understand that they can take a position with respect to the information they uncover in sources—that a stance is required. We are not necessarily creating scholars, but we are trying to develop critical thinking skills. Students' thesis ideas are original (even if scholars have long ago arrived at them) because they come from places inside themselves.

There is also a confidence issue here that I encounter in another form when they arrive in a college composition course: this sense that they are not scholars, and, therefore, that their criticisms hold little value, as though they have no right to assess the text in any meaningful way. Embedded within this is a palpable fear of being wrong. Students want to be told how to understand a text, rather than wade through it on their own and make discoveries about it. These students are afraid of risk, for fear of being incorrect. As teachers, we must tell them that writers aspire to critical discourse and an original interpretation from among the myriad possibilities, so that they know there is room for diverse views.

Clearly, Shakespeare was not writing for the Harvard scholars (indeed, we are told that the groundlings reacted most volubly; clearly, they got it)—an anachronistic argument—but students understand my point. Scholars do not own the literary canon, though, of course, they can offer specialized understandings of it. Novelists, playwrights, poets are attempting to reach a larger audience, to share their insights into the human condition, so readers (audience) can take away something from their original work. Student writers begin a dialogue with the text—they answer the authors back—*yes, I see it your way, but . . .* And it is in this conversation that they "research" their thoughts, discover their voices, their vision, distinguishing a common and a unique experience of the world.

Teaching Students to Think Originally

In teaching students how to write, we ask students to think for themselves. We require use of the imagination in early student writing, which is generally more creative and informal. As students move up in grade level, we begin to demand more formal writing of them, and this is where we sometimes move away from creativity into the stilted regurgitation of the ideas of others. Culling facts from a text or several texts is certainly an admirable skill, but it must be set apart in the process and, ultimately, secondary to the process, as part of the process and not an end in itself. If we purport to create critical thinkers out of our college-ready student population, then we have to require the higher level of thinking that is achieved through the simultaneous processes of analysis and synthesis.

We need to help them *originate* thesis claims. They may encounter the same thesis in a critical essay (written by a scholar), but if they arrived at this central idea through a dialogue with the literature (*King Lear*, *Beloved*), then it is their own: it is their contribution to an understanding of the novel, poem, play. If they do encounter a thesis in a scholarly work that is a mirror of their own central idea, they need not panic. Obviously, others before them have arrived at a similar understanding of the litera-

ture. It should be flattering to see that they have a valid understanding of the text. The scholar's work may now be used to
enhance their own central argument. As long as they arrived at it
firsthand, directly, then they need not be concerned. They can
produce their freewriting to exonerate themselves. If, however,
they read the critical/indirect/secondary sources first, they have
arrived at a thesis secondhand: it is not of their own generating;
this is clearly plagiarism. We must encourage them to move from
responding to primary source to freewriting original responses
to researching of secondary sources (in that order).

Students need to break down the texts for details, recognize
them as relevant to their focus on a particular topic, and then
pull them together under the all-encompassing thesis idea. The
paper itself is a balancing act of interpretation and evidence. We
are not asking for opinion separate from evidence. We are not
asking for evidence separate from what we no longer call opinion, but interpretation. An academic argument is an interweav-
ing of both evidence and interpretation. Many student essays are
heavy on one side or the other: that is, they are either largely
opinion without any grounding in sources of information, or they
are merely literal, factual restatement of source material without
any insight. These imbalanced essays need to be discussed with
students so they recognize the favoring of one over the other in
their own writings.

Certainly, writing is a means of communication, a way of
sharing ideas. Research requires that students gather in the voices
of others: the scholars, specialists, experts. We need to teach students to synthesize secondary materials within their own inter-
pretative arguments: now the field of discourse has widened to
encompass voices beyond the primary sources. What chaos—what
noise—what frenetic energy to be controlled on the page, har-
nessed (so that it does not pull the paper in a hundred different
directions) for the framework of the student's own construction.
No wonder students are overwhelmed. Look at how many voices
threaten to submerge that of the student writer. Even an experienced researcher wrestles with the voices and ideas of the outsider. We must begin to teach them how to exert control over the
chaos—how to shape an academic argument.

Clearly, the student voice must be the predominant voice. It is her or his paper after all. Teachers of English can help by teaching paraphrasing and summarizing skills. Students do not realize that they should quote only with a purpose in mind—when there is poetry and elegance in the phrasing; when there is power in the prose; lastly and most simply, when they cannot say it better than the original author. Quotes should be saved for the eloquent and profound. We must advise students that they should quote primary sources more often than secondary ones. They should quote the poem or the play because they should ground their readers in the text; this is where most of their evidence should come from. It is the artistry of the original that should resonate in their papers—the language of the primary—the words of the play, poem, novel. It is Proust's, Dickinson's, Dostoevsky's, Joyce's, Woolf's words that should linger in the minds of the student writers and the readers of the student essay.

Students should be encouraged to overcome the temptation to simply copy information from secondary sources, because comprehension is more likely to be accomplished if they paraphrase and summarize. If they can put information into their own words (paraphrasing and summarizing), they are demonstrating understanding of that information. Paraphrasing and summarizing require more engagement than quoting. Copying is easy. Students often copy entire pages (which they could have photocopied and pasted into their note journals more easily and with the same amount of success in terms of increasing their understanding of content). Obviously, in this electronic age, cutting and pasting is a simple task. If, in haste, a student forgets to cite the source of the quotes (cut and pasted materials), they are plagiarizing.

The secondary sources bolster a *student's* central argument; they should not overwhelm it. The primary sources should be quoted more often than the critical secondary ones, which are easily paraphrased and summarized (after all this is a critic, not a Shakespeare, not a Churchill, and his or her intriguing understandings of Shakespeare can be put into the student's own language more easily). Students need to know when it is appropriate to summarize, paraphrase, and quote. We need to encourage them to make these distinctions.

In integrating secondary source materials, students should have made selections based on their own interpretive positions. They should know how useful the reference will be—how relevant, in terms of the framework they are constructing. They must not make the error of believing that the secondary sources create this framework: if they do, they have failed the research assignment: the paper will come from somewhere outside of themselves—they will be distanced from the subject, disengaged from the project. If we as teachers accept this as research, we will have failed them in the process.

Why We Do Research

Research writing maintains the contact between accepted knowledge even as this knowledge is filtered and challenged through a unique point of view. It offers communication of ideas, a chance to respond, to confirm, to deny what is written. Through these reactions, researchers contribute to the ongoing dialogue on the subject matter. *Research* is inherently unending: answers to research problems are often acknowledgments of complexities and are not fully resolvable. It is innate human curiosity that we want to engage. Students want purpose and meaning when they are sent off to find information. We must make the experience meaningful for them. We must whet their appetite to know and to understand. It is not merely the opening of doors to knowledge: it requires focusing the discerning eye and stimulating the logical brain.

Teaching students to respect the process of research prepares them not only for the global experience, but the individual one. It defies ignorance; it breaks through preconceived notions and moves them toward enlightened understandings. We must teach them to value the process as much as we have encouraged them to value its product—knowledge. Research can engender dialogue across centuries, across oceans, through infinite cyberspace. It represents a human desire to move forward, to discover new places and fathom the nature of "self" in the process. It breaks through isolation to dispel ignorance, prejudice, fear of the unknown; to challenge the untestable and blindly believed, corruption, and manipulation. In its expansive nature (because it is an endless journey and simultaneous journeys at once though time, space, and self), it protects against threats to human liberty. Research is at once accepting of the individual voice and tolerant of multitudinous voices. It imposes further questioning, generating hyperlinks that descend through layers of space.

The "show me, don't tell me" nature can be tapped into to encourage students to explore knowledge and arrive at understanding. The lethargic self remains tied to long untested beliefs. Teach students to shed that skin, leave it behind, and embrace the human need to understand.

Research is never a rote process. If we lose sight of its significance, how can we expect our students to embrace the process willingly?

Through pursuit of knowledge, and I do mean *pursuit* (not a *handout* of information), we can find both answers and questions. If you take exploration of self out of the research process, you limit your students to reporting. Exploration involves questioning, challenging, testing—not merely absorbing information. This desire to understand beckons us further; it synthesizes the past to the present and future. It embodies the creative as well as the logical processes of the mind. We cannot encourage students to remain fixed to the page of information without questioning, challenging, engaging, responding. If students respond in subjective papers, then they are equal to the task: they face it eye to eye and are not afraid of the truths it holds, or does not hold, for them.

CHAPTER TWO

First Things First: Emphasizing Primary over Secondary Sources

The Argument for Emphasizing Primary Sources in the Process

In the English Classroom

Writing the term paper in an English class involves immediate immersion in primary source materials. Teachers of English assign the reading of the novel, play, poem—one type of primary source material—before allowing a student to research the background of the author, or the historical context of the novel, or the literary themes of the novel. So, students of English typically have immediate access to primary source materials, whether they recognize this or not—even if the teacher does not identify the literature itself as a primary source. Students writing literary analyses requiring research have an advantage, then, in formulating their own ideas with respect to firsthand information—before reading critical, secondary materials. This is an ideal setting for authentic research; that is, if the student has not read criticism (scholarly or oversimplified online notes) before reading the novel, or alongside the novel.

Often, though, the potential for an authentic research experience goes unrecognized by both teacher and student. This occurs when teachers direct students to secondary source materials too early in the process, before students have fully responded to the primary sources; that is, before they have had any insights into the literature. This chapter focuses on the importance of freewriting in allowing students to explore their own ideas before they are influenced by the experts, by secondary sources. As part of a progression forward into the integration of external

sources, freewriting works to establish student voice and vision—
encouraging authority in both.

Class discussions, personal responses— all contribute to students' understandings of the text. Students often see this as separate from the formal task of writing about the novel, play, poem;
viewing their ideas about the text as valid in this forum, but not
in their writing. These students choose, in writing, to consult the
"experts," online study guides. They turn off their own ideas in
the writing process, even when they have been engaged in class.
The connection between original claims offered in class discussion and literary analysis in writing needs to be more overtly
forged. Many students believe that a term paper is dependent
upon ideas imposed on it from outside themselves. They have it
backwards: they research the ideas of others first and then attempt to write "original" thesis ideas ("original" understandings). The irony of this process seems to be overlooked. Clearly,
this approach to research needs revisiting.

If, in the process of writing a term paper in an English course,
we stress research of secondary sources first, we are tempting
students, if not setting them up, to plagiarize. They will encounter criticism that they will not be able to separate from their own
ideas about the text: novel, play, poem, film. Then, the confidence issue takes over: how could their ideas possibly be as valid,
as significant, as those of the published critics? Even students
who try to separate their ideas from those of the critics (the students who recognize that their integrity as writers is at stake here)
will have been corrupted by what they have read. Critical sources
will clearly influence the thesis idea. In a worst-case, though common, scenario, they will present the idea of a critic as their own
in a thesis—they will not even recognize this as plagiarism: "I did
not take it word for word!" They will read condensed versions
of literature online, and some will intentionally, others inadvertently (because the ideas have entered their consciousness), appropriate these themes and present them as their own in thesis
statements. Some students will actually (nobly) cite the source of
the idea (they do not usually do this if they have taken the idea
from an online study guide, like GradeSaver, because they recognize that the teacher will be horrified). It is disconcerting for teachers to see a source citation (scholarly or otherwise) after students'

"thesis statement." It clearly indicates that students do not understand that academic writing requires student writers to offer their own interpretive stance, that a thesis statement must originate with the writer.

Their reading of surrounding texts (prefaces, introductions, critical annotations) will also influence students' points of view. They will tell you that they did not understand the text: please do not accept this from them. Encourage them to go back to the literature and read it again, to freewrite a response to the book, to study it more closely and arrive at original understandings, even if they are imperfect understandings.

Conferencing with students who have difficulties understanding the literature will allow you to pull from them. If we do not feed them ideas and take steps to prevent their finding feeding sources, students will have to have their own ideas. (Reading comprehension skills may be weak in some students, but that is another book, focusing on another aspect of teaching English.)

As teachers of English, as avid readers, and as lovers of the written word, we are often so smitten with our own understandings of literature that we can overwhelm our students. I always tell my students that I am not so egotistical as to desire my own ideas back at me in their essays. Though I model interpretive reading skills, I do not wish to encounter my ideas in their writing. I want to know what they see in the readings. I want them to recognize that they can have well-reasoned understandings. Many students have astonished me over the years with fresh insights into texts I have been teaching for decades. I have had to catch my breath on a number of occasions. This is wonderful. This is ideally what we seek to achieve: student engagement with the reading—critical discourse at all levels of understanding. Not all of our students can enlighten us, but all of them can be challenged to have their own ideas about what they read.

THE FIRST ASSIGNMENT: FROM FREEWRITING TO THE CRITICAL ANALYSIS ESSAY

Begin with freewriting in response to the literature (primary source)—a full week of freewriting, of exhausting all ideas on the literature assigned. The goal is, of course, for students to

---

The Progression from Freewriting to Formal Writing

1. Have students freewrite for several days in response to the literature (primary source)

2. Have students pull out a central idea from the body of their original freewriting

3. Have students *precisely* articulate the original thesis (the all-encompassing central idea)

4. Have students skim (or reread) the literature for support of their central argument

*5. Have students generate an outline (this is a creative process and should involve several attempts at placement of ideas for a dynamic organization)

6. Have students compose the essay

Note: Freewriting, in conjunction with outlining, should cut down on the number of rough drafts a student writes—though it will not, of course, eliminate the need for revision.

---

land on the thesis idea, to have an insight into the text that can be fashioned into a central claim. This delving beyond the topical, this exploration beyond the ordinary, will help them eventually write the "A" essay, the outstanding essay. In their freewriting, students should be encouraged to take interpretive risks, to go beyond the obvious in their understandings of the literature. Within these writings (journal entries in response to the assigned reading) students experience both the emergence of their own interpretations through an authentic dialogue with the text and the organic process of shaping their ideas. The landscape of freewriting is without parameters; it is self-generating. Students literally, concretely, follow where their thoughts lead them. They are not bound by form, which can limit the expansive nature of thought. Form (rhetorical strategy) is coming into existence through understandings of content and, therefore, derives from thought rather than imposes on thought.

Once students pull a central idea from their freewriting, have them determine that it is not merely a competent or an obvious understanding of the literature. If the thesis is sophisticated, direct them back to the primary source to skim it for supporting evidence. There is no point in crafting an argument for which there is little or no evidence (if the interpretation embodies an admirable but ultimately insupportable risk): it will degenerate into opinion without proof. What we are after is an academic argument, a balancing of interpretation (insight) and detail (example). If they cannot find the evidence they need, then they should be encouraged to return to the freewriting stage of the process as their interpretive risks cannot be substantiated.

Honing the thesis is the next step. Consider having students write several versions of the same central idea, perfecting their constructions and their diction each time. If they begin in a heavy-handed fashion with a construction that is some version of the statement "This paper will prove that . . . ," you can ask them to lop off the unnecessary phrasing, though there are numerous examples of published writers who favor this sort of emphasis in the showcasing of thesis through language, as opposed to placement. (Formulaic placement—that the thesis must be placed as the last sentence of the first paragraph in the essay—should not be required of students. The thesis will be most effectively showcased if it functions as an organizing principle in the essay: this is its purpose. Read the essays of professional writers, of scholars and specialists, and you will see that you rarely find the thesis in formulaic location. A thesis can appear anywhere in the introduction. And a thesis, if implied, need not make a physical appearance in the introduction, but manifests from the logic of the presentation of points in the body and is revealed in the conclusion.)

Teachers need not insist that a thesis be a single statement. If we read published writers' essays, we often see that one sentence will not suffice. A single statement is wonderfully concise, and that aspect of it need not be overlooked, but there is a danger of oversimplification in a single statement, a resolving of all the complexities of the work under analysis into a single statement. There may be layers to be treated in an analysis. As long as the thesis represents the synthesis of points offered in the essay, it is correctly wrought. In Raymond Williams's essay "New English Drama," he builds a thesis in layers, moving from general to more specific statement of intent:

My own impression of the last six or seven years of English drama is of a period of extreme confusion and eclecticism, made more so by a genuine burst of vitality and energy. I do not think we can begin to understand this period unless we put it in the context of the general development of drama in this [twentieth] century. (26)

In an essay I wrote on Mary Cassatt, I created a layered thesis, but I moved from specific to more general: "Rather than paint the sacred, or beloved object, Cassatt chose the more elusive individual. Sentimentality and illusion are absent from her work" (123).

Notice Williams's use of first-person voice and my use of third-person voice. Voice selection is a stylistic choice: one we should consider allowing our students to make in the crafting of a thesis statement.

You will find that professional writers often have a thesis paragraph, and that each subsequent sentence refines the previous one in a narrowing down to the focal point. Here is an example of a thesis paragraph from Mark Stevens's essay "Goya's Third of May, 1808."

Both are extraordinary paintings [*Second of May, 1808* and *Third of May, 1808*], *Third of May*, however, has attained an importance beyond what is customary for great works of art. It is a painting of archetypal significance, a picture that seems to signal an essential change in the temper of Western civilization. Many observers have called it the first modern picture. They are right, not because Goya's formal approach was innovative, although it was, but because he was the first to portray, without false consolation, the horror near the modern heart of life. (Stevens 451)

This building to a focus occurs within a separate paragraph of the introduction, after background (or a definition of terms) has been accomplished in the initial paragraph (though it can precede background and definition of terms—writing is never a formula).

The list thesis, a favorite of students, is not the most sophisticated embodiment of a central idea. It reflects a lack of true synthesis of the ideas the student is presenting in the body of the essay. It indicates that students are aware of the points they will consider in the body, but it does not demonstrate that they understand how these points are related to each other. They are listing but not processing: we must require students to forge connections, as this facilitates comprehension and an understanding of relationships among ideas. Making connections encourages coherence in the paper. The list thesis is consistent with the reporting mode; it does not indicate the assimilation mode. It is topical and for this reason should be discouraged.

OUTLINING

From the identification of a central idea, which students glean from their freewriting, have students generate an outline of relevant points. To a certain extent, this should come organically from the freewriting—the imprint of organization may already be appearing in the freewriting. If students cannot see this, or if students are having difficulty with form, you can conference with them and help them identify the landscape of their ideas, which is the beginnings of design, of form.

You can also encourage students to experiment with several versions of organizing thought through outlining. In the most blatant approach to this, have them consider using the strongest point of the argument as the first paragraph of the body. Then have them refashion the outline using the weakest interpretation first, building strength in their argument as they move forward in the presentation of ideas. Placement of points involves logic, but it is also a creative step in the process of writing and reflects some stylistic choices. Organization can and should involve creative expression for a more subtle and more imaginative approach. An essay can stand out in a pile of essays, as a result of its compelling and unique organization. As teachers of composition, we understand the importance of rhetorical strategies in the instruction of writing—how organization is connected to originality in writing.

A formal outline is not necessary; bulleting and "asterisking" are sufficient. I often ask students to generate three versions: three possible ways of placing points relevant to thesis on the page. Students can play with rhetorical strategies—comparison/contrast, description, cause and effect, narration, analysis, synthesis. I ask my students questions and suggest responses along these lines: *Do you want to examine a motif in the literature?* If so, then you are *synthesizing* elements of the work. *Do you want to compare a central image of the text to the theme?* Then, you are creating a backdrop and doing a subtle *comparison/contrast* essay. *Are you focusing on a particular characterization?* Then, you are *analyzing*.

I have my students make two copies of one of their outlines. Then, I do something I also do in my creative writing classes with poems: I have them cut one copy of the whole work, in this case the outline, into pieces: they cut out the separate points. I should say that the outline is in its barest skeletal form when we do this, without evidence as yet. Then we throw the separate points, the shreds of paper, on the floor in reckless abandon. Naturally, students love this. I have students randomly pick up points and glue them down onto a clean blank page. We examine the results: students will get some nonsensical results, of course, but they may also get a juxtaposition of points they would not have placed in sequence before this exercise. Once again, we are injecting fresh perspectives into the process that they normally find dull and, as a result, often skip.

We have to break down conventional thinking, which leads to tedious writing. Creative outlining is an illustration of how to break it down. If student essays are organized more creatively than the convention, they will stand out. Originality comes not just through the generation of a sophisticated insight (thesis idea), but from the form it takes as well—just as it does in the visual arts. Students who are in rehash mode will often follow the novel's plot in a conventional mode of organization. This lends itself to plot summary and creates the most predictable, most prosaic approach to organizing the essay on literature. You have probably received many essays organized in this way, with lengthy passages of plot summary. Students often do not know that there are other ways they can organize their thinking on a topic. Provide them with options to consider: teach them rhetorical devices and model a creative outlining process. Form, as much as content, can offer their papers the distinction of originality.

Considering the Evidence in Composition

Once students have generated an outline of their own interpretations, they are ready to consider the evidence. Evidence should be selected to support points, but finer lines need to be drawn. They should not select quotes that restate facts they provide in the essay (through paraphrasing). For example, if a student is writing about Poe's "The Fall of the House of Usher" and he or she writes that Roderick's physical appearance is pale and corpse-like, the student writer should not follow that detail with a quote from Poe that describes Roderick's "cadaverousness of complexion" (Poe 259) because the student has provided a fact from the story that needs no corroboration (he or she has paraphrased Poe)—not to mention the redundancy issue. Students need to understand that they should integrate quotes to be used in supporting claims (interpretations). If a student makes the claim that the tarn in Poe's story is a passageway to dream (to an alternate reality), he or she has offered an interpretation that now must be supported by evidence from the text. The narrator speaks of impressions that are dreamlike and hallucinatory, in fact, he states that "when [he] again uplifted [his] eyes to the house itself, from its image in the pool, there grew in [his] mind a strange fancy — a fancy so ridiculous, indeed, that [he] but mention[s] it to show the vivid force of the sensations which oppressed [him]" (Poe 257).

A critical essay is a dialogue of insight and evidence. As they enter the composition stage, they must synthesize through a balancing of interpretation and detail. If the essay is heavy on detail, they are writing reports. If the essay is heavy on interpretation, then they are writing mere opinion. Teach them to write an academic argument.

The Second Assignment: Modeling Academic Writing

The next writing assignment will move toward writing the traditional research paper and build on the previous assignment (literary analysis essay). After students receive a grade on this first essay, I hand it back to them to use as a framework for the next assignment, the first research assignment.

I have students find a published critical essay (must be scholarly, must be from a legitimate database) on the literature they evaluated in their own critical essays. The scholarly article will serve as an organizational model for student term papers. They print out or photocopy the scholar's essay. I have them ready it for a class presentation: they will mark up the text of the article based on assignment specifications to follow. Students will be asked to analyze essay structure (as well as content).

To clarify this assignment, before continuing with students' own structural analyses of published literary criticism, I insert this lesson, using art criticism. I select a work of art so that I do not need to introduce a new work of literature (because of time constraints) but, more importantly, because visual analysis is often more understandable for students in a discussion of the subjective writing process (which must balance interpretation against evidence; that is, subjective stance against objective detail).

Students analyze a color plate of Goya's *Third of May, 1808* (via the overhead) as their primary source. Then, I use Mark Stevens's essay, "Goya's Third of May, 1808" (via the overhead) to provide a model for analytical writing. The essay has the skeletal framework of argument (found in most academic writing) and relies heavily on description in the organization of the body (obviously, because in art criticism, one would expect the primary rhetorical strategy to be description—the rendering of the visual image in language). What follows are some examples of what I emphasize in a study of Mark Stevens's criticism.

The final layer of the thesis of Stevens's essay is the statement "[Goya] was the first to portray, without false consolation, the horror near the heart of modern life" (451). This is the essence of the central claim because it embodies an interpretive stance to be supported with evidence from the painting, in the body of the essay. In trying to determine the thesis of the essay, many students will look to the conventional placement of the central idea, to the last sentence of the first paragraph. If they do, they will read the following: "Goya commemorated the event in two large canvases: *Second of May, 1808*, which shows the mob attacking the Mamelukes, and *Third of May, 1808*, which portrays the execution of the hostages" (Stevens 451). Clearly, this is not the thesis of the essay: these are facts—indisputable. Here, in this particular statement, no argument is offered. This information is obviously background, used to inform the reader about what is literally revealed in the paintings. The reader needs these historical and artistic facts to understand the interpretation that follows. The thesis is brought into focus in the last sentence of the second paragraph in this essay, where a subjective, not an objective, statement is made: "the horror near the heart of modern life" (Stevens 451).

Stevens describes the painting, providing evidence for claims made in the body (which are relevant, of course, to the thesis idea). In one description Stevens writes, "The light contains no spiritual overtone, but rather emanates from a common lantern; an intense glow is cast on the small, grisly scene, but it cannot pierce the dark reaches" (453). This is an example of impressionistic (somewhat subjective) detail. The diction used by Stevens slightly corrupts objectivity. His use of adjectives tinges the description, makes us see the visual (the painting) in a particular way; it is a detail, but a detail enhanced with impression, which is always subjective. He imposes his vision on the reader: we see the painting filtered through Stevens's lens. Here is an example of pure description from the same essay: "[The central figure's] outflung arms are mirrored by those of the corpse in the foreground" (Stevens 453), a literal truth, a fact.

Making the distinction between detail (evidence) and claim (interpretation) is crucial. Students often do not see the difference until they have some practice in making this distinction for themselves. I ask them to scan two body paragraphs, highlighting the objective material (details, facts) only. The students are then asked to identify the subjective material (claims, interpretations) that these details are supporting. They may need to practice this several times before they appreciate the difference. I also vary this by asking for an outline of the critical essay with points creating the framework and evidence of the content, in fairly conventional outline form. Students cannot shape an academic argument—an intermeshing of claim and evidence—unless they understand how interpretation differs from fact.

In modeling the difference between interpretation and fact and the more subtle distinction between pure description and impressionistic description, we move toward teaching students a basic understanding of critical thinking and its application in writing: how writers manipulate through language choices, how critics take and maintain a subjective stance. We move forward on two fronts here, teaching them to be discriminating readers (they recognize how language can manipulate), and we show them how critical writing is accomplished.

I use popular journal articles as well as scholarly articles in modeling essay structure, particularly for topic-directed writing and for personal essays. For modeling organization of scholarly works, I recommend making several anthologies of criticism accessible in the classroom. Collections edited by Harold Bloom (available in most local libraries) can be used to demonstrate the form that criticism takes.

After the lesson on the structure of academic argument, students present a scholarly article on the primary source they read for the first writing assignment (the literary analysis essay). I do this informally: we are all seated in a circle, and I ask students, in turn, a series of questions to guide their presentations. First, I ask for the scholar's thesis. Students will often find that the thesis is more than a single sentence. Sometimes they will find that the thesis is implied, rather than explicitly stated, and that they must look to the conclusion for a concrete version of the central idea. I advise them to look to the title of the essay for a reflection of the central idea. (We know this, but often they do not know what is so obvious to us.)

Second, I ask them to determine the skeletal framework of the argument, to find the points that are offered in the argument (in the body of the essay). I review the difference between point and fact. I have them identify one interpretation and one fact supporting the claim they have isolated. I remind them that some facts can be impressionistic, embodying a critical stance in their statement of "truth." Can they identify these subtleties?

Third, I ask them to note the construction of the scholarly essay as a balancing act of claim and evidence. For the most part, they will observe the scholar engaged in a dialogue with primary sources—examining passages of the literary work and responding fully to those passages as they are made relevant to the organizing principle of the essay, the thesis. They determine if interpretation is balanced against detail; assessing whether or not

---

Analysis of a Scholarly Article

Have students do the following:

1. Identify the scholar's thesis

2. Discuss the outline underpinning the essay

3. Note the balancing act of detail against interpretation in the body of the essay—the dialogue between scholar and primary source(s)

4. Evaluate the scholar's integration of secondary source materials into the framework of original argument

5. Determine rhetorical strategies in the essay's organization

6. Identify structural boundaries: where the introduction ends and the body begins; where the body ends and the conclusion begins

---

the scholar ultimately convinced them, as readers, that his or her stand was valid. In arriving at an answer to this question, evidence provided in the body of the essay clearly plays a crucial role. Have students consider whether or not the scholar took risks that were insufficiently supported by textual evidence. Have them consider why the scholar did not rehash the plot—how the scholar expects her or his audience to be familiar with the primary source(s). (If the scholar has inserted some plot summary into the essay, students should consider the purpose served—background, continuity of understanding.)

Fourth, I ask students to evaluate how the scholar integrates secondary sources into her or his own argument and to consider the place they hold within the framework of the scholar's argument. Here I want them to determine how often primary sources are used over secondary sources. I also want them to look at the physical ways outside sources are used—does the scholar summarize, paraphrase, or quote sources? Obviously, an experienced writer is utilizing several ways of integrating sources. Have students determine how fluidly sources are woven into the scholar's own argument.

Fifth, I ask them to identify rhetorical devices (modes of organization) used by the scholar and to note the relationship between content and form. I want them to hypothesize on other rhetorical devices the scholar could have used and why the scholar chose a particular device to organize evidence and interpretation in the essay. For example, if the essay considers only Poe's "The Fall of the House of Usher," then the thrust of the essay is most likely analysis—a breaking down of story elements to understand theme. If the writer incorporated Poe's other works, then the thrust would most likely be synthesis—an uncovering of preoccupations and obsessions of the author, tracing themes or motifs in his works. What is the critic's purpose? How does form underscore it? Through close study of scholarly essays we model and introduce possibilities for organization the students have never considered before.

Sixth and last, I ask them to delineate the sections of the essay—where the introduction ends and the body begins, where the body ends and the conclusion begins—noting the purpose of each section. What is accomplished in the introduction: historical background? definition of terms? specific example that will broaden out to a thesis? How long is the introduction? Through examination of published essays, students will see introductions of more than a single paragraph. I have my students look at essays that have three paragraphs, eleven paragraphs, and two paragraphs of introduction.

Although it is not a scholarly essay, here is an example of an outstanding introduction of two paragraphs in length from the personal (but also expository) essay "Black Men and Public Space" by Brent Staples:

> My first victim was a woman—white, well dressed, probably in her early twenties. I came upon her late one evening on a deserted street in Hyde Park, a relatively affluent neighborhood in an otherwise mean, impoverished section of Chicago. As I swung onto the avenue behind her, there seemed to be a discreet, uninflammatory distance between us. Not so. She cast back a worried glance. To her, the youngish black man—a broad six feet two inches with a beard and billowing hair, both hands shoved into the pockets of a bulky military jacket—seemed menacingly close. After a few more quick glimpses, she picked up her pace

and was soon running in earnest. Within seconds she disappeared into a cross street.

That was more than a decade ago. I was twenty-two years old, a graduate student newly arrived at the University of Chicago. It was in the echo of that terrified woman's footfalls that I first began to know the unwieldy inheritance I'd come into—the ability to alter public space in ugly ways. It was clear . . . (34)

The second paragraph continues, but I ended the excerpt of his introduction with Staples's thesis: "to know the unwieldy inheritance I'd come into—the ability to alter public space in ugly ways." This is an interesting introduction to show students for several reasons. It engages the reader immediately with vivid writing, and it moves less conventionally from specific to general (the illustration leads to a broadening out of inference: "to know the unwieldy inheritance [. . .]—the ability to alter public space in ugly ways"). This introduction also invites the reader into a seemingly confessional piece, but ultimately it exposes the reader to self-recognition (even self-confession): how ready he or she had been to believe Staples was a criminal and not a victim. Furthermore, this introduction embeds the thesis in the second paragraph, the central idea following a dash. As most student essays move conventionally from general background information to a specific thesis, it is important for them to see other ways of setting up an introduction: from a grippingly precise example to a broader statement of purpose.

Have students account for the differences in length of introductions. Some writers need to provide lengthy backgrounds for their topics to establish their central claims. The introduction is a foundation for the thesis idea: it must provide the necessary support—how much information is needed to do so will vary from essay to essay and will be determined by the thesis idea.

In the eleven-paragraph introduction mentioned earlier, the writer confined all of her secondary source materials (studies by other educators in her particular case) to the introduction. This established solid footing for the body of the essay, which was exclusively an evaluation of primary source materials. Most research papers provide a balancing act in the body of the essay between original ideas, primary sources, and secondary sources. This writer's organization was unusual because she was taking a risk in her thesis and needed to connect herself to authoritative studies to establish continuity of understanding in her field. Her thesis needed to rest on these other sources. Her essay is what I would call "top-heavy" and an interesting, unconventional way to organize a research piece.

After evaluating introductions, have students look at the transition from introduction into body. Within the body, they should examine transitions between paragraphs—how effective transitions work the thread of the central idea through the fabric of the body.

Last, I have them determine where the conclusion begins: I have them identify the restatement of the thesis idea, the revisiting of an examination of purpose, and the offering (in sophisticated essays) of a final insight. In Mark Stevens's essay on Goya, he restates his thesis metaphorically and uses the construct of a question: "What could be more intimate than the cold prick of a rifle against a white tunic?' (454). This restates the central idea, "the horror near the heart of modern life" (451). His final thought has to do with Goya's revelations of intimacy and in the conclusion leaves readers contemplating Goya's *Naked Maja*, "one of the most erotic pictures ever painted" (Stevens 454). Stevens forges this final connection—Goya's inevitable intimacy with death that culminates an intimacy with life.

This assignment—the structural dismantling of an essay— models organization. Students recognize that ideas are not haphazardly abandoned on the page by the writer. It concretizes expressions of form (of organization). They see overlap in rhetorical approaches and an overall framework created by the organizing principle of the thesis idea. They have been exposed to the integration of the voice of the outsider; scholarly essays always incorporate secondary sources in the analysis of primary ones. Students will think about what they are doing when they enter the synthesis stage of research writing, when they are confronted with the voices and ideas of outsiders and must consider how these external sources will fit into their own vision of the subject. The published critic has demonstrated this dynamic for them. They will embrace the idea that writing is not a formula— that they can place the thesis anywhere in the introduction (or not, if it is to be implied). Students will observe less obvious approaches to restatement of thesis in the conclusion. They will see less predictable approaches to synthesis—to fluidity in writing through generating transitions more creative than "in addition" and "finally" (which are brittle, contrived expressions) among ideas in the body of the essay. They will notice a balancing of detail and claim. They will note brief quotes and lengthy quotes and the writer's rationale in quoting fragments or complete sentences. Students will see the relationship between content and its rendering in form.

Students present this evaluation of the scholarly essay in class. They then see how many different and valid ways literature can be interpreted. There is no single, correct way to understand a masterpiece of literature.

This evaluation of criticism serves as a research task (finding a scholarly source—using a database—not a mere search engine approach), a modeling of form for a literary analysis essay (with secondary sources), a demonstration of the myriad interpretations of a single work of literature—that there exists more than one valid way of understanding art, literature, music.

THE THIRD ASSIGNMENT: MOVING FORWARD INTO INTEGRATION OF SECONDARY SOURCES

The Progression from Freewriting to Formal Writing

Have students do the following:

1. Freewrite for several days in response to primary sources to generate an original framework

2. Compose a literary analysis essay, analyzing *only* primary source materials

3. Evaluate a model of academic criticism through presentation of a scholarly article

4. Integrate secondary sources, expanding the original literary analysis paper into a term paper

---

Now students are ready to integrate secondary sources into their own essays. Allow them to use the essay they have already found on the literature (used in their presentations). Ask them to find four or five additional secondary sources (they do not all have to be scholarly articles; students should determine what is appropriate and relevant) to include as well. This is an effective approach to writing the research paper because each stage has had purpose and meaning. The stages taken have lessened the temptation to plagiarize because students already have their own idea (evolving thesis) and a framework into which they can work the ideas of scholars and specialists. Students are now more capable of considering ways of integrating sources: when it makes sense to quote and when it makes sense to paraphrase (as a result of their earlier evaluation of a scholarly essay).

The composition of the research paper, the culmination of this process approach to research writing, becomes an exercise in synthesis. Students must make some elbow room for the ideas of others. This practice has several benefits: they learn that theirs is the predominant voice and vision of the essay, because their thesis remains *essentially* the same and is, therefore, original; second, research enhances rather than submerges their ideas (and language). This assignment reinforces the validity of students' own central argument and discourages plagiarism of others' ideas.

There are several ways to consider the integration of secondary sources. Many students may be tempted to look for criticism that is an exact match and then simply insert quotes into the literary analysis essay they wrote earlier in the process. This is the easiest and least critically engaging approach to the assignment. (Because they are being redundant and because they are just using the exact language of the critic, they are not delving deeply into the research stage of the process, and they are clearly not having a meaningful research experience.)

My recommendation is that students should go back to the outlining stage of the process, keeping the thesis virtually intact and deciding how the secondary source material fits into the argument already shaped. Does the critical material compliment or refute students' claims? Does it extrapolate their claims? Does it restate their claims? Each student must make these distinctions.

Tell students that they need not find exact matches to their own points. They are probably not ready to refute the ideas of scholars (though some will admirably try), but they can forge their own connections, bridges, using criticism that is not so direct. For example, if they are writing a critical essay on Poe's "The Fall of the House of Usher," they may use criticism of one of his other stories, "Ligeia," which they can connect to "The Fall of the House of Usher." In this case, they will be connecting the criticism of one work to another of Poe's works and synthesizing material in the process. This is more sophisticated than simply pasting quotes of criticism on "The Fall of the House of Usher" into an essay: to merely paste requires no thinking, only exact matching. (Student may not even fully understand what they are cutting and pasting.) Consider requiring a student analyzing one Poe story to rely exclusively on the criticism of another of his writings. This would be more challenging and considerably more rewarding for both teacher and student.

Students need to understand what kind of information can be applied and how it is appropriate. Students writing a term paper on Capote's *Other Voices, Other Rooms* may never encounter Sam Howie's article "Character, Caricature, and the Southern Grotesque" in the *Writer's Chronicle* (February 2005), because they have narrowed the search for sources too precisely. In the article, Howie does not consider Capote (he considers Faulkner and O'Connor, among others), and yet much of the article is obviously relevant to an essay analyzing Capote's writing in connection and in distinction to other southern writers and as it defines and analyzes the southern gothic novel (the broader categories). Students would have to bridge the gap—connect the description of southern grotesque sensibility to Capote's particular voice and vision, moving from the general to the specific, and forging their own definitive connections. What students would be required to do in this circumstance is more sophisticated because they are overlaying the article—applying the broader definitions to a specific work, to which they most certainly apply. Here students are using their own critical thinking skills to see a relationship. This is certainly more sophisticated than simply using critics to restate the ideas at which the students have arrived on their own. If students search too narrowly for articles that only treat *Other Voices, Other Rooms*, then they miss out on synthesizing and having a complete understanding of Capote's unique artistic vision in the context of the southern gothic style and the even broader topic of Gothicism. Certainly, broad can be good, if it is applied to the specific. Too specific can be limiting—students may find they can access (at their school or local library) only one article that considers Capote's *Other Voices, Other Rooms*.

Broad can be dangerous, though, because it can cause students to miss the target of their thesis idea. Broad can turn into filler: students may take materials that do not apply to the focus of the essay. Students then write a survey piece that is topical and wide and vague. Often, this is a result of too little time taken to formulate an original approach to a topic, and as a result, students cannot see how information connects to the subject or how it should be organized in a research paper. Students do not have an organizing principle at work in the process. They cannot synthesize because they are in copy mode. We need to put students into analysis mode.

Have students submit the resulting critical essay, which incorporates some secondary sources, as their first experience using indirect/evaluative external sources in composition. Naturally, all outside sources must be documented both in the text and in the bibliography.

Through this approach, as opposed to the conventional progression from note-taking to the final term paper, you will have given student researchers a template for a process that encourages original thinking as the first step in the foraging for knowledge among sheaves of paper and layers of meaning.

Other Classrooms, Other Subject Areas

In courses other than English, the research paper is often assigned in a way that encourages the culling of secondary sources as a first step. This is unfortunate because it implies that this is the first step of the research process, when it is not. *The research problem exists in the primary source material more than it exists in the secondary source material.* Preliminary assignments involving the use of primary sources (lab experiments, diaries, letters, interviews) should be given before allowing access to secondary sources.

Encourage students to read some firsthand accounts (even if the jargon overwhelms them, they can wade through some of the material). They will gain an appreciation for the primary studies and an exposure to the passion and energy revealed in the firsthand research that may be missing from the secondhand sources. After all, the secondhand source is an indirect source of information: a filter has been applied, the language changed to the evaluative—these language changes have an impact.

Require students in all subject areas to freewrite their responses to the primary sources—whether lab data, interviews, firsthand accounts of scientists or explorers, letters, photographs, artifacts—to write informally as they try to sort through their understandings of a research topic. Encourage students to brainstorm in writing. This is part of the process of problem solving, envisioning through the lens of unique perspective. Let them work through the information in trying to evaluate it.

Clearly, without reading and without incorporating secondary source materials, research papers would have little or no validity. Students as researchers must defer to the experts, but they should not refer to secondary sources absolutely (nor initially). Undeniably, research of secondary sources is crucial to the education of students. They will learn (in-depth) about their topic from secondary sources, scholars or specialists in the field who evaluate primary sources. This is a body of information that will feed their papers. But they need to be receptive and awake to process it. They need to have first made their own observations about the topic to recognize connections and distinctions with respect to their own ideas—initial ideas on the topic in response to firsthand accounts or in response to their own observations (experiments, studies of human behavior). Firsthand knowledge prepares them for secondhand knowledge. Is there a consensus of opinion in the academic community on the work of a pioneering scientist—if not, why not? The experts can be used to support original points, *enhancing and enlarging, and often correcting, the student's interpretations*. Expert sources give the paper credibility and speak to the continuity of understanding in the field and to the truth (knowledge) of human experience and existence, but their role, by definition, is secondary. The student needs to synthesize both primary and secondary sources in the process of the evolving thesis idea.

I recognize that immersion in primary sources is not an easy first step in some disciplines. Students often have very limited access to firsthand sources. They do not have access to archival materials; they can only conduct rudimentary science experiments in the lab. Nevertheless, some correlation between the tangible and what many students conceive of as the abstract (because it is in print and far removed from them as part of its secondhand nature) needs to be generated by the teacher. As we know from our own teaching experiences, students benefit from the hands-on approach to instruction more than they do from behaving as sponges, absorbing lectures on a topic. As Hamlet observes to Rosencrantz (who is clearly corrupted by influence), "When he needs what you have glean'd, it is but squeezing / you, and, spunge, you shall be dry again" (*Hamlet* 4.2.19–20).

Ryan and Ellis's book *Instructional Implications of Inquiry*, published in 1974, advocated creating an environment in class-rooms for inquiry-based learning—"[t]he instructional proposal that students question, analyze, and even generate knowledge, as well as receive it" (Ryan and Ellis vii). I think most teachers embrace this approach to instruction, but, oddly, we do not seem to insist on these directives when assigning a research paper: that students must analyze as well as collect information. Ryan and Ellis remind us that most of the subject areas we teach have "parent disciplines" that offer a methodology as well as a body of content knowledge (5). Are we only to require the documentation of an understanding of content without the documentation of the understanding of the skill—the ability to both find and evaluate information (methodology)? In addition, the skill (process) will be a lifelong practice even as the content (knowledge) is often forgotten. Students will always have access to information, to knowledge—what to do with that content material is what we must teach them. In discussing the sciences (social studies and natural sciences), Ryan and Ellis explain the "two fold structure composed of (1) its procedures or methods of inquiry [. . .] and (2) its main ideas and major concepts [. . .] The first facet of structure is concerned with the *process* of scientific investigation, the second, with the *products* of investigation" (Ryan and Ellis 5). They note that in the conventional approach to instruction, teachers merely glean knowledge from secondary sources for the purposes of educating students—essentially, transferring knowledge (6). Ryan and Ellis acknowledge that though product remains important, of equal importance is process, "an understanding of how the products are generated" (6–7). Give students authentic research experiences by requiring them to use inquiry in response to primary materials in the generation of a paper that is more than a fact-finding, fact-absorbing exercise. If you insist on a subjective stance, you foster independent learning and lifelong learning.

I must juxtapose my emphasis of primary sources over secondary ones, in the initial stages of the research process, against Walliman's opposing emphasis of secondary sources at the same stage of the process. In his book *Your Research Project*, Walliman argues,

> Secondary sources are invaluable in the early stages of research, when you [the researcher] are exploring a subject and seeking problem areas. It is difficult to see how anyone could dive straight into effective research using only primary data sources and ignoring the theoretical or empirical work of others in the same or similar area of study. (199)

His is a compelling argument, but I think until student researchers have an established voice and until those student researchers have cultivated a sense of authority of authorship and an understanding of validity in original understanding, they are entering a lion's den of danger—to be swallowed whole by the experts or authorities. If not a den of lions, it may be one of luxury where temptations of worldly experience and knowledge and comforts entice: information offered up on a plate. Secondary sources must, of course, be consulted, but for the high school student, in particular, the stage at which they are consulted in the research process is of crucial consideration.

Indirect sources, expert or critical sources, Walliman tells us, provide the background (knowledge base of the subject area) and the research problem (20–22, 199). The individual research must be meaningful within the body of existing knowledge. I think that our apparently different emphases are not mutually exclusive because Walliman speaks of the framework of subject (the research area), and I speak of the framework of the individual project, which requires the subjective eye. Although it is true that in the beginning stages of research, one must not "ignore the theoretical or empirical work of others," this early exploration of secondary sources is more to be practiced among college students than among high school students, where the challenge to authority needs to be cultivated, the right to question authorities needs to be sanctioned. When students become true researchers, when they are writing contributions to academic understandings, they will then be able to discern that the subject area context is the backdrop for the original argumentative stance—that it colors, adds dimension, may even give the illusion of stability in the fashioning of the thesis idea. It is primary source material that provides the answer to the research problem—in part, or imperfectly, or inconclusively (certainly in no oversimplified way) for the individual research project: it is primary source material in which the thesis is grounded. If secondary sources are the backdrop, the drama is played out on the stage, in the dialogue the writer engages in with his ideas and props (literally his evidence, substantiation) parading across the platform. The proscenium of the paper or project must be the researcher's, or what is the point—if just to duplicate what has been done before.

Walliman recommends several approaches to identifying and developing a research problem: "to find a question, an unresolved controversy, a gap in knowledge or an unrequited need within the chosen subject. This search requires an awareness of current issues in the subject and an inquisitive and questioning mind" (20–21). It is the negotiation and dialogue among researcher, primary sources, and secondary sources that becomes the project.

Walliman offers advice in avoiding pitfalls in the construction of a research question, which he says "arise mainly from the failure to grasp the necessity for the *interpretation* of data in the research project" (22). What he enumerates in his list of "four common mistakes" are certainly danger areas for most high school students. He includes self-serving research ("an excuse to fill in gaps in your [student's] own knowledge") and oversimplification, where the final answer indicates that there is no "why" to the problem to begin with (22–23).

Training students to transcribe information only, to organize without having an organizing principle, encourages an incomplete process. We are not asking for objective writing in a research paper. We need to recognize this. We are asking for objective research to be conducted, but the resulting paper will be subjective. We *are* asking them to be impartial in the process, at least initially, open- and broad-minded to the information on the topic that is out there and to take a balanced approach to the information in the beginning, but, ultimately, they are required to take a position (subjective writing) with respect to the information, facts, they find. If we ask them to report only, the research process is unfinished. They have only found and copied information: they have not analyzed it. We must require understanding—comprehension—as part of the process. There will be a certain validity in the process, even if the product is an imperfect understanding or analysis of content. Engage the human mind—do not program a machine.

Social Sciences

One of the most compelling arguments for emphasizing primary over secondary sources of information comes from the preface of Boyer and Nissenbaum's *Salem Possessed: The Social Origins of Witchcraft*. The book originated from an undergraduate course they were teaching at the University of Massachusetts in Amherst to give "students the opportunity to explore a single event in depth through the careful and extended use of primary sources" (ix). Unexpectedly (because they were researching a subject almost three centuries old—one would have thought the subject was already thoroughly exhausted), this is what happened, in Boyer and Nissenbaum's own recounting:

> what had started purely as an interest in experimental teaching soon assumed a scholarly dimension, as we became aware of an immense body of unexplored documentation about Salem Village, the community in which the witchcraft outbreak first erupted. For example, in the archives of the First Church of

Danvers, Massachusetts (the direct descendant of the "witch-craft" parish of 1692), we found extensive records for both Salem Village and its church from the founding of each [. . .] which included community votes, tax assessments, and lists of local officials. Here, we soon realized, lay buried far more information about the civil and ecclesiastical history of the Village and its inhabitants *than was to be found in any existing historical account of the background of Salem witchcraft.* (emphasis added, ix–x)

If researchers take in only secondary or indirect sources of information, they expose themselves to the possibilities of incompleteness, of biases, whims, agendas, contexts (what Boyer and Nissenbaum refer to as "intellectual autobiography") of the intermediaries—all of which are considered at some length in their preface in reviewing some of the secondary sources (and the context of their own book). Boyer and Nissenbaum provide a good illustration of this:

Even Upham's analysis [*Salem Witchcraft*], however, impressive as it is, remains incomplete and ultimately unsatisfactory. Like most nineteenth-century local historians, Upham idealized the sturdy colonial yeomen who figure in his narrative, dwelling almost affectionately on their petty disputes but often drawing back from confronting the larger patterns implicit in these disputes or from analyzing them in serious political terms. (x)

And they trace the reliance of other researchers on this seemingly definitive source: "Of the modern historians of Salem witchcraft, the few who have discussed the pre- or post-1692 situations at all have continued to rely uncritically on Upham's imperfect narrative and analysis" (xi). It is easier not to question, of course, just as it is easier to compile indirect or secondary sources in the research paper. Let us not encourage bad habits. Apparently convenience and, dare I say, naïveté can cause inaccuracies to appear even in the work of scholars who do not challenge but accept without question.

Students need to learn the importance of primary sources early on. I am talking process more than product here. I am not saying that at the secondary school level we have to discover what others before us have or have not discovered at higher levels of academia; what I am saying is that the knowledge of process is often more important than product. Lay the foundation for challenge and open up the possibility for discoveries.

In history, a student could obviously explore interviews, diaries, letters, articles—*contemporaneous* with the historical event. Once students have some contact with firsthand sources of information, they can begin to make up their own minds about how to approach the subject and take risks in their understanding of a topic.

Students need to identify what they have discovered through the primary source experience of interviewing a Vietnam veteran, for example, and compare/contrast this against what the history books and scholarly articles tell them about soldiers and their experiences in Vietnam. The foray into primary sources will have prepped students well for their adventure into secondary ones. They will automatically compare/contrast findings from both research approaches. The difference is that now they are more open to critical thinking—reading secondary sources with a more discerning eye, more likely to question, to compare/contrast, rather than simply collect and copy scholarly information into a paper (the cut-and-paste method).

The importance of framing content within analysis is emphasized by Glenn Whitman, an Advanced Placement U.S. history teacher, in the instruction of process.

> Teaching students how to be and think like historians is my fundamental goal for each of my secondary school history classes. But when I begin each course by asking, "What does a historian do?" I am often amazed by the difficulty students have in answering the question. Considering how history continues to be taught, their reaction is not surprising. My students have to learn that history does not center on the memorization of dates and names from textbook readings. High school history classes should be balanced between providing historical context for understanding contemporary issues, while at the same time serving as "ground zero" for the training of future historians and history teachers. (469)

Whitman assigns an oral history project as a way of providing students with primary source material as an opportunity to "directly engage with those individuals who were makers, or part of history" (470). More important, he observes, "From their first introduction to oral history, students immediately realize problems associated with it and, like all historical sources, oral history needs to be validated by other forms of historical reporting" (470–71). Here is the attempt at reconciling primary and secondary sources of information, the beginning of contradiction without which there can be no true synthesis. Without this dialogue, without this level of engagement required of students, a research project assignment is of little educational value. Of final note, he observes a general absence of such requirements from history instruction "because of a perception that a multi-skill project is an unrealistic expectation for amateur student-historians. This, however, is an underestimation of the valuable history that can be produced when even unseasoned student-historians are schooled in the methodology of oral history" (474).

Clearly, primary sources offer students the research problem that will shape their thesis ideas and create the framework of response (argument). In the article "Implementing Assessment and Improving Undergraduate Writing: One Department's Experience," Olwell and Delph consider the generation of a thesis statement as an important part of the research process and note that students often do not.

> Part of this problem is the result of their [undergraduates'] general intellectual development, and many students enter even upper-level classes with what educational researchers call a concrete level of analysis. That means in their history classes they are still convinced that history essentially consists of names, dates, facts and events, all of which can be easily classified as true or false. It is part of our job as historians to combat this tendency and to show students that the best practitioners of history view the study of the past as a series of problems that must be analyzed critically to ascertain the central issues and motives that shaped events, ideas and peoples' actions. (par. 9)

A thesis is a subjective stance. Require students to take a position with respect to the facts they are culling from sources, both primary and secondary. Research instruction should be aligned with your inquiry-based approach to content instruction in the classroom. Inquiry demands an answer that embraces complexities and that requires interpretation of the evidence.

SCIENCES

In science, it may be students' own lab experiments that will serve as jumping-off points. If the experiment (with students' limited access to materials and their lack of expertise) only accomplishes a review of scientific method, it will have served a purpose, reminding students that "[s]cience works with testable proposals" (Gould 417). Gould, paleontologist, educator, and writer, tells us that "[s]cience, in its most fundamental definition, is a fruitful mode of inquiry, not a list of enticing conclusions. The conclusions are the consequence, *not the essence*" (emphasis added, 417). Again, process over product: this is the recurring theme in research. Gould, in his provocatively titled essay "Sex, Drugs, Disasters, and the Extinction of Dinosaurs" exhorts, "If the growing corps of popular science writers would focus on *how* scientists develop and defend [. . .] fascinating claims, they would make their greatest contribution to public understanding" (417). Gould is a master of making both the processes of scientific inquiry and scientific knowledge accessible. Content knowledge is inextricably linked to process.

In his article "Writing as a Tool for Learning Biology," Randy Moore notes, "Truth in science is the product of argument and persuasion, which, in turn, are created with language." Argument is not created through objective restating, but through critical thinking. Students must be able to interpret information, to make sense of their observations, through both analysis and synthesis of data. Argument requires the integrating of interpretation and evidence: it is not pure observation. Moore cites data from *Consumer's Research*, which shows that "[a]lthough 59–65% of high school students can do an adequate job of informative writing (i.e., describing what has occurred), only 7–25% of students can do an adequate job of analytical writing (i.e., describing why something has occurred; Anonymous 1987)." This is a symptom of students' topical approach to both learning and research as seen in all subject areas. This lack of engagement engendered from reporting only is certainly cause for concern. Randy Moore is correct to point out that students who cannot generate argument in their writing will be at a disadvantage when pursuing professional careers. In addition, he recognizes that using writing to assess content knowledge is less valuable than using writing to facilitate content knowledge. The first benefits teachers; the second benefits students. The first is product oriented, and the second is process oriented. Randy Moore emphasizes "the power of writing as a tool for thinking about, understanding, and communicating ideas." He also recommends that teachers encourage students to read literature in their fields (beyond the science textbook) to teach content, but also to model "effective writing."

In distinguishing between "correct writing" and "effective writing," Randy Moore describes both types: "correct writing" masters writing conventions but is often overly formalized and ultimately inaccessible; "effective writing," on the other hand, "uses familiar words, avoids inflated phrases, and uses shorter, more forceful sentences." Clearly, if we seek "effective writing" from our students, we must encourage understanding of content beyond mere regurgitation of information from textbooks. Dialogue writing or freewriting in response to lab work or other primary source materials could help students arrive at an understanding of the subject matter, through exploration of their own responses to observations made during hands-on experiences or to other primary materials.

Writing examined as reflection is offered in a model of extension by Richard A. Huber and Christopher J. Moore. They maintain that "the presentation of science as a process of following step-by-step instructions and filling in blanks on worksheets promotes erroneous and impoverished concepts regarding the nature of science." This type of response—to direct questions (which, by the way, encourages fragmented thinking often presented concretely in sentence fragments)—is clearly limiting. Huber and Moore have observed, of worksheet assignments, that "most problematic [are] the written directives [which] deprive students of ownership over their investigations. Rather than designing and carrying out investigations to answer their own questions, they are following instructions to find out if they guessed the correct answer to the teacher's questions." These assignments hinder original thinking that would move in its own direction, if left to the blank page. Of note, also, is that providing ownership works in opposition to appropriating the ideas of others (plagiarism). The programmatic experience, the worksheet after the lab, is analogous to the book report assignment used in the instruction of English literature, which takes away ownership—does not require ownership of ideas because retelling is circumscribed by the narrative. We need to allow students to have ideas that they arrive at on their own, without corruption by absolute direction (any outside source, including the teacher): let students create their own understandings, let them discover the organizing principle and test it through exploration of primary sources, let them discover both the evidence and the underpinnings. Huber and Moore believe that although both writing and discussion are integral through the entire process of inquiry-based learning, writing is most important in the synthesis stage, "when students have a more comprehensive collection of experiences to reflect upon," close to the end of the process.

When Primary Sources Are Too Abstruse

In papers in fields like science and social science (less true in social science), information for a research paper will, by necessity, come largely from secondary sources (availability, accessibility in terms of understanding). For example, papers written by scientists (primary sources) describing their studies and including their results will often be too abstruse for high school students. Students should begin with these sources, though. Give them a chance to wade through them before exposing them to secondary sources. Later in the process, students will be reading the indirect source, the textbook writer, the popular science writer, who is making the scientific information accessible. High school students are limited in these fields of study: they cannot conduct sophisticated experiments, cannot survey large populations. As a result, learning is accomplished through reading about the studies of experts translated into the vernacular. It is through synthesis of these that a student can arrive at an original stance, at a thesis. The student must be informed (have read the secondary materials) in order to evaluate and take a position. The high school student of science and social science (unlike the student of humanities, who can more easily access primary sources—in art, literature, and music) must often use these secondary sources in creating a central idea. In these fields, synthesis becomes almost more important than analysis in forging an interpretive argument in a paper. Students must review the data and look for points of intersection and divergence. In these papers an important part is the introduction, which is a launching off pad, providing cited authorities for the smaller voice of the student to come (in the statement of thesis). In the thesis, the student responds to these heavyweights—the secondary sources—the indirect voices that make the direct sources comprehensible. (In papers written in the humanities, the heavyweights are the writers, artists, composers, who speak directly to the students, without intermediaries.)

Finding Sources

Naturally, students are more comfortable retelling, relying heavily on description (observation) without analysis. The hardest task in reporting is finding sources, not thinking, not analyzing. Often, students incorporate the irrelevant in their panic to fill up the paper. It is a relief to find a whole book on the topic. Students visibly sigh, relaxing when they have one or two books on the general topic. Often, they cannot discern what is relevant or irrelevant in consideration of their particular approach to the subject: they are not sure which material in the text belongs in the paper and which is not precise enough for their own topic idea. Part of the problem is, of course, that they lack a focus to begin with because they have no way of generating an original framework (subjective stance), which would allow them to discriminate, selecting appropriate and relevant materials. They go broadly into the topic area without refinement, without acknowledging shades of meaning, or without the recognition of the resonance of ideas in harmony.

This is why sources listed in student bibliographies are similar in kind and few in number: students do not know exactly what they are looking for. They have not generated parameters. Barbara Valentine, in her article "The Legitimate Effort in Research Papers: Student Commitment versus Faculty Expectations," illustrates the difficulty college students have in both defining and then in accessing appropriate sources. Valentine, in her observations, found

> students often used very chaotic, what they themselves termed "random," methods for finding materials for their papers. A characteristic comment was: "I felt kind of aimless, kind of like shooting in the dark, you're going to get something eventually" (Junior, Sociology). In addition, the process of finding sources took lots of time, time many of them had not bargained for, leaving them discouraged and wearing down their resolve to do a good job. A student remarked: "I was glad I found something and didn't really care how good it was" (Senior, Social Work).

Valentine's article focused on miscommunication or lack of communication between faculty members and students: students were not clear on "what the professor wanted" (Valentine). According to Valentine, "students' understanding of the purpose and expectations of the particular research assignment usually varied with what many of the course professors expressed." As teachers, we need to define research in general and then explain it in its particular connection to our individual assignments. Students will then be better prepared and less frustrated by the prospect of finding appropriate sources and later understanding how the sources are to be used—hopefully, they will be used within the design of a subjective stance.

Students believe that they cannot reach original conclusions in research papers. They always surrender their minds to the authorities, to the secondary source materials, paying homage by allowing these authorities to write their papers for them—summarizing and paraphrasing at best, quoting at length at worst (if we are not considering the potential for plagiarism as well)—their voices willingly submerged to the voices of outsiders. Obviously, they are not (always) capable of authoring the same ideas as the experts, but certainly they can engage in some discourse with them. Students need to be more confident of their own place in the paper: they need to understand the subjective design that takes shape during an authentic research experience.

Conclusion

Teachers must make the distinction, as students are not always aware of the differences between primary and secondary sources. We must expose students to both forms of research, if we are to cultivate critical thinking in all disciplines. We do not emphasize critical thinking if all we require is organization of secondary source information. Some students barely skim the secondary materials they find. They organize a report that has not been viewed through the subjective eye. Secondary sources are meant to teach and inform, but without engagement through exposure to primary sources, we may not be able to teach students to utilize secondary sources correctly, as enhancement to their own positions in response to limited forays into primary sources—scientific, historic, literary.

Critical analysis mode can be achieved through use of primary source materials. Have students list observations of the scientist, inventor, philosopher, world leader, historical event, experiment; have them react in the form of freewriting; that is, have them engage in a dialogue, through their own writing, with the primary source(s)—have them respond to the ideas and findings of the scientist, philosopher, or historian. Use freewriting to catalyze form and outlining to engage both logic and creative energy. If you do not encourage engagement with primary sources in the form of free writing, you are likely to get a recopying of facts and details from secondary sources without insights: this "recopying" is not "research." If you first place students in the library, requiring them to collect secondhand information, you are only teaching them to report: you are directing them to remain outside of the information, discouraging them from engaging in a dialogue with it. As teachers we must establish the groundwork for authentic research in our disciplines.

Working Definitions of Plagiarism

Plagiarism takes two distinct forms: source of information and source of language. Both types are serious offenses—the first appropriates the ideas and information of others without proper acknowledgment, while the second uses the scholar's, writer's, or expert's exact words without proper acknowledgment (thereby taking the *expression* of the ideas from a source). Often, source of language plagiarism is unrecognized by students, who have provided a parenthetical tag, citing the source of information (of ideas). But because they have not properly paraphrased the material, the rendering of the ideas may be identical or nearly identical to the wording of the original writer. As a result, the parenthetical tag alone is not sufficient acknowledgment.

Of the two types of plagiarism, source of language is often overlooked in instruction on avoiding plagiarism. Because of this, I begin my discussion with this form of plagiarism.

Source of Language Plagiarism

Source of language plagiarism is presenting someone else's language as one's own. Students who plagiarize in this way will extract whole passages or partial passages of text(s) and attempt to pass them off as their own writing. These students are essentially quoting without using quotation marks. It may, or may not, be the result of pure carelessness; the student has forgotten to enclose the material within quotes, and the language and sentence structure match the original exactly. This is obviously plagiarism, whether intentional or not. But we also have source of language plagiarism when only minor changes have been made to the original—a word here and there, with the sentence structure of the original left largely intact. This is usually the result of poor para-

phrasing: the student does not understand how to correctly paraphrase the language of the scholar or specialist. In identifying
this kind of plagiarism, you will find that the writing is resonant
of the original in sentence pattern and diction: often, a few words
have been changed by the student, typically through a plug-in
approach, but the sentence structure mirrors the original, and
much of the language of the original has not been changed. Again,
even if this appropriation of language and sentence structure is
followed by a parenthetical citation, it is still an instance of plagiarism: the parenthetical citation documents *source of information* only; the tag makes no claims about the language of
expression. Quotation marks (or setting off the quote from the
text of the paper) are necessary to indicate that exact language
has been used—for so it has, with some slight and ineffectual
modification. To correct this, students have two choices: they
can quote exactly (without any modifications) and use quotation
marks (or setting off the passage) to indicate that the material is
directly extracted, or they can correctly paraphrase the material,
rephrasing the material so that it is irrefutably written in their
own words. Of course, sources must be documented for all quotes,
paraphrases, and summaries integrated into student writing.

Students need to use quotes around complete and partial
quotations—exact diction from the original text. I encourage the
integration of partial quotes when students cannot phrase a word
or expression more effectively than it is expressed in the original.
They should be encouraged, though, to put most of the language
into their own words; after all, this is what paraphrasing involves.
When they do not paraphrase correctly, there are a variety of
clues we can spot: sentence structure presented will be more sophisticated than their own; awkward (often archaic) plug-in words
from the thesaurus will flash like neon signs; uneven writing will
be the final result. These poorly unified constructions should stand
out against the backdrop of their typical writing style. As an instructor, when you suspect source of language plagiarism, you
need to check the original source (probably, it has been parenthetically cited for your convenience) and compare the two passages. Then, you need to conference with the student. Be prepared
to define this particular form of plagiarism for the student and
provide examples of correct paraphrasing.

Intentional Source of Language Plagiarism

If a student is intentionally, rather than inadvertently, plagiarizing language, then this student should, obviously, be addressed firmly. Direct them to a college site on plagiarism, such as OWL (Online Writing Lab at Purdue University)—located at http://owl.english.purdue.edu/handouts/research/index.html—to ground them in the evidence that this lifting of language and sentence structure is absolutely unacceptable. They should be made aware, as well, of the penalties colleges impose on plagiarists. If an entire paper has been purchased or taken from an online site (or from anywhere else for that matter) then this is clearly a blatant case of plagiarism and must be dealt with according to school policy. In all likelihood, you will have to track down the source yourself (typically, it will be a single source) using a search engine method to find the original material (see Chapter 6). Online study guides may also offer one free essay, or a tempting passage of an essay, for a variety of literary texts.

Inadvertent Source of Language Plagiarism

Often, though, source of language plagiarism is unintentional: students have not been taught how to properly paraphrase another writer's language. These students, who extract language without using quotes, will usually cite the source parenthetically, documenting the sources they have used for information. Unfortunately, they do not recognize the error they have made regarding the language of the source. If they do not use quotes to enclose the extracted material, they are presenting the wording as their own. At this juncture, I advise students to decide to meticulously quote (using quotation marks) or to correctly paraphrase the language. I allow them to make the choice.

Quoting should not be overused in a paper: eventually it becomes filler and submerges the voice of the writer. Students should quote when they cannot effectively translate the energy or beauty of the prose. It is the primary source—the literature—that should be quoted most often, not the secondary sources: the critical sources are more easily paraphrased. It is largely a response to the primary source that makes the student essay original. It is important to keep this in mind.

Selecting to paraphrase, rather than to quote, accomplishes several tasks: one, it allows the voice of student writers to remain consistent in the paper (the essay is not a collection of critical or scholarly voices—voices of the outsiders); second, it allows for greater fluidity in terms of the organization of papers; third, it demonstrates comprehension of material—students cannot possibly paraphrase what they do not understand. This is the most important point to emphasize to students: on some level their avoidance of correct paraphrasing reflects on their comprehension of the source material. Paraphrasing indicates to the teacher that students have fully understood the secondary source information; indeed, they have understood it so well that they can recast the ideas of the scholar or expert.

In fact, an inability, or an unwillingness, to understand secondary source material is probably the main cause of a proliferation of filler quotes in students' essays. They are sending us several possible messages—one, they truly do not understand the subject material; two, though they have a handle on the subject overall, the writing of some of the scholars is too abstruse for them; three, they are too overwhelmed to think—it is easier to copy word for word. This unwillingness to analyze results in an imbalance in the body of the essay—it is full of quotes that are often illogically strung together with little back and forth dialogue between student writer and quote; lengthy quotes are pasted in, often without surrounding text by the student to justify their inclusion. The student who recognizes that it is wrong to fill up an essay with quotes may still paraphrase incompetently.

Students generally use the exact sentence constructions of the original and simply insert synonyms in place of words they edit out "to make the passage their own." Students often begin this plug-in method in grammar school: to change the language of the original, they use the dictionary to find synonyms and then insert them. I was never given any formal training in paraphrasing in my entire academic career. It is absolutely necessary that we teach this skill along with the research process. We need to separate it out; consider allotting at least one class session to the practicing of correct paraphrasing. Paraphrasing is a skill that is not easily mastered, and yet few of us separate it out and teach students how to accomplish this balancing act of meaning and voice. When separating it out, I suggest that it is practiced within the meaningful context of their research projects—connected to a larger assignment; otherwise, it is piecemeal instruction.

TEACHING PARAPHRASING

In teaching students how to paraphrase, I tell them to put the text aside for a few moments and try to remember what the writer said—the ideas, the insights. Then I ask students to try to write down these ideas. I have them compare the two versions, their translation with the original text. Integrity of ideas must remain intact. If student writers change the meaning, then they will have to try again. If they, unintentionally, appropriated exact language, then they will have to try again. If students are unable to remember what they have read, then they should view the passage as a whole and synthesize the main points in their own words. Encourage them to change sentence structure, in addition to altering diction. In changing language choices, they should try to use their own words, before consulting a dictionary or thesaurus. Students who have established voices will have an easier time doing this. Eventually, all students will learn how to do this to some degree of proficiency. Can you understand what the writer is saying? Yes?—good, now try to put it into your own words. Vary sentence structure, vary diction, but do not vary meaning.

Here is one of the examples that I use at the high school level when teaching Poe's "The Fall of the House of Usher." This original passage is from Patrick F. Quinn's *The French Face of Edgar Poe.*

Original Passage

But the narrator of this story does not come upon the conditions of everyday life at Usher's house. Rather the reverse: he has left everyday life behind him when he enters upon a scene in which decay and death are the presiding elements. His lapse is into a dreamlike state, and a hideous veil has been let down rather than removed. However, it is only through the wrenching effect of paradox that the baffling complexities of his state of mind may be conveyed. (239)

Source of Language Plagiarism

The narrator doesn't find the everyday at Usher's home. Instead the reverse: he left ordinary life behind when he encounters a scene in which decomposition and death are the commanding elements. His passing is into a dreamlike mood, and a horrible veil has been dropped not taken away. Yet, it is because of the wrenching impact of contradiction the perplexing complexities of his mindset may be related. (Quinn 239)

The example of source of language plagiarism is the kind of plagiarism English teachers encounter regularly. The translation makes little sense and is jarring because of strange word choices (students make use of an online thesaurus—usually, the most common synonym is selected) coupled with the sophisticated sentence structure—the use of a colon in this example. The sentence patterns of the original and the source of language plagiarism passages are identical, and the final product (source of language plagiarism) is disjointed and lacking in clarity. It is an incomplete union of two voices; of course, it will leap off the page as an aberration.

An Example of Correct Paraphrasing

The narrator of Poe's story has left the ordinary to find the extraordinary in the House of Usher. A decrepitude of spirit and body overwhelms his expectation of the everyday. The veil Poe describes as having been drawn aside has fallen into place so that, through it, the narrator enters a dream. The subtleties of the narrator's hallucination are revealed through Poe's use of contradiction. (Quinn 239)

Here are some examples from a student paper on *Vanity Fair*. This student is to be acknowledged for her attempts to paraphrase and summarize the material from critical sources on Thackeray's novel, so that her essay is not merely a collection of the voices of the outsider, a collection of quotes. Readers will observe how challenging it is for students to both fully comprehend and then adequately rephrase the ideas of the scholars or experts. Clearly, students need to practice paraphrasing and summarizing as separate exercises (within a larger context) before we ask them to incorporate the ideas of secondary sources into their papers. I hope what follows makes a good case for what I am recommending.

In this first example, the student uses the plug-in approach, coupled with exact quoting of a part of the passage, to serve as a paraphrasing of the original source, a critical essay by Dyson. Though this is not a source of information issue, for the student provides the parenthetical citation of author's last name and the location of the material (she references the page number), this would be an example of source of language plagiarism. This is the student's phrasing: "Thackeray understands the inner thoughts of his characters, and he is responsible for telling the audience what these are (Dyson 74)." This is Dyson's own language: "knowing his [Thackeray's] characters' secret thoughts, and telling us what these are" (74).

In this next example from the same student paper, you can see that some attempt is made to paraphrase correctly, though it is not fully accomplished. In Kettle's essay we read, in his description of Thackeray's point of view in *Vanity Fair*, "Everything depends on the capacity of the novelist to encompass in his own personality an adequate attitude to what he is describing" (15). In the student essay we read, "It is the responsibility of the artist to weave into his work his personality and attitude, and Thackeray succeeds in doing so with his characters (Kettle 15)." Again, we get the parenthetical tag at the end of the paraphrase, so that source of information is not the issue. Here the student is clearly trying to rephrase Kettle's point and some comprehension of meaning is coming through, though there is also a tampering with meaning. "It is the responsibility" is somewhat presumptuous of Kettle's intent, and the student is misunderstanding: Kettle's comment is about perspective/tone in the novel, not about the author's injecting of his own personality into his writing.

Next is an example of summary, where there is a condensing of information. We see a layering of interpretation and some miscomprehension over this as well: it is not completely pure in terms of summary or paraphrase. This is the student's writing: "Thackeray strived for reality to be conveyed through literary devices, and thus, through questions and interpretations, he allowed the presence of reality to overwhelm his novel (Tillotson 54)." Here is Tillotson's own phrasing:

Through it he openly admits, as no modern novelist dare, *all* the relations of the novelist to his story. The novelist does write what he knows to be "terrific chapters," he does construct and manipulate his characters, and he is also carried beyond his conscious self [. . .] He remembers, and observes; he is affected, as he writes, by what is happening around him—the unwritten parts" of novels. Thackeray's candour about all this is part of his love of truth. Believing in truth, he can afford to admit that what he writes is fiction. (54)

These examples show the challenges students face in paraphrasing and summarizing in maintaining integrity of meaning, in using their own voices as writers, and in methodically citing the sources. As teachers, we clearly must spend time on these skills, in discrete exercises, within the authentic context of the research assignment.

Correct paraphrasing requires the preservation of the insights and ideas and evidence of the writer. It demands that students must process these ideas, insights, and evidence and then synthesize through use of their own language. Because the paraphraser is synthesizing, the sentence structure will change. Students should not regurgitate, but should comprehend and document this understanding through the process of absorbing and regenerating.

There are a number of fine academic websites that provide examples of correct paraphrasing and compare it to outright plagiarism of language. The Nesbitt-Johnston Writing Center of Hamilton College in Clinton, New York, offers a link called "Writing Center Handouts" (http://www.hamilton.edu/academics/resource/wc) and provides information on "Using Sources" (https://my.hamilton.edu/academics/resource/wc/Using_Sources.PDF), which your students will find very helpful. Another excellent site, mentioned earlier, is the Online Writing Lab at Purdue University or "OWL" (http://owl.english.purdue.edu/handouts/research/index.html). This site encompasses all elements of process and covers documentation styles very well.

I recommend that teachers have students select a paragraph of criticism (which students have accessed for their research paper) to paraphrase, as an exercise initially separate from the process of composing the research paper; isolate the skill for a day or two. Once teachers remove the pressure of having to do this for immediate incorporation into the paper (along with the necessity of doing several paraphrases and summaries at once for the research paper), students can focus their energies on learning the skills of paraphrasing and summarizing. After allowing time for all students to attempt this, read over their paraphrases and select the strongest example of correct paraphrasing to share with the others. Have them critique the paraphrase. Have the student whose work was selected discuss the process of creating the paraphrase. Instruction can also be organized as a collective experience. Students, in groups of three or more, can work together on paraphrasing a passage from a critical source. You can also connect this activity to a work of literature you are already reading and actively analyzing in class, so that the criticism will make sense in light of class discussions about the text. The most important objective to reach is the recognition that paraphrasing is the ability to restate someone else's ideas in one's own language: it is a by-product of understanding the critic's or scholar's thoughts. If it is done well, a bond is established between the writer and the interpreter.

Source of Information Plagiarism

Source of information plagiarism is a more familiar form. This is typically what students understand as the definition of plagiarism—the appropriation of the ideas, thoughts, and evidence of another writer without proper citation. It can be intentional or inadvertent. This kind of plagiarism is grounded in insecurity and carelessness. Students believe that because they are not authorities, they cannot possibly contribute to knowledge on the subject—let others have the ideas. Online sources, prefaces, introductions, anthologies of criticism, and teacher's interpretations all seem fair game to these students in their hunt for the theme of the book they are required to analyze. Often, they are not content with merely landing on a central idea, "their" thesis idea, but they will take several points and will not synthesize these several points under an all-encompassing central idea; that is, they will sometimes pick one of the interpretations to serve as the thesis and use the others as points offered in the body of the paper. These ideas may not be directly related to each other, but separate understandings, other ways of understanding the literature. They do not recognize how disjointed the body of the essay is when they attempt to create an essay out of these distinct claims. These inherently weak approaches to essay writing are easily discoverable because they are often illogical in terms of organization yet at the same time sophisticated in terms of diction. A more challenging case in identifying plagiarism comes from the student writer who has taken the entire pattern of point and evidence from another source—from online sites or from analogous printed versions, such as *CliffsNotes* or *Monarch Notes*.

Intentional Source of Information Plagiarism

These students suffer from lethargy or worse. They do not believe it is wrong to appropriate the ideas of others as a way out of thinking for themselves. They somehow convince themselves that by placing these outside source ideas into their own words, such ideas become their own ideas; they almost forget later that the ideas originated elsewhere. In the case of lifting whole papers off an online source, there is obviously no thought given to academic integrity.

Identifying source of information plagiarism can often be difficult; we are harder pressed to document it. Usually, though, a pattern emerges: the claim offered and the evidence provided by students may be a duplicate of the presentation of ideas and evidence made available on an online site (even if they have scrambled the language of the original to disguise this theft of ideas). Ironically, these students are fairly good paraphrasers (or proficient users of text scramblers): they have to be to avoid detection when they are presenting someone else's ideas as their own. They realize that teachers will be using online search engines to find exact matches in language and sentence structure and partial or lengthy quotes of an online source. Note that students who do not normally balance detail against interpretation— that is, students who usually do not write academic arguments— may suddenly offer you a perfectly balanced body of material. Trace the pattern back to its source. It is usually an online source of information (more readily accessed, requiring less effort). The language may be the student's own (in the case of our savvier students, we sigh, regretting that they did not put this much time into understanding the literature!), and it will be harder to find an exact match when you do a search engine check. But the pattern may be there intact: this particular point followed by this particular item of evidence. Students will often go back to the primary source for the full-length quote rather than use the partial quote version usually offered on these online sites.

Inadvertent Source of Information Plagiarism

Ignorance can be slightly to blame: students do not recognize that taking the ideas of others is plagiarism if they have translated these ideas into their own words. These students will properly cite sources after all quotations included in their papers; they recognize this as correct form. These same students, who zealously cite sources for quotes, do not understand that paraphrases and summaries must also be documented in their essays. Ideas become appropriated through this transference to student language. Students have lost track of boundaries—where their voices and ideas end and the voices and ideas of the scholars and experts begin.

As regards the gray area of common knowledge, I advise my students that if they had to look the information up in some text (article, book, documentary, interview, radio program), that source must then be documented. Common knowledge widens with education and experience. They have not arrived there yet. Sources must be cited for both information (facts, details) and ideas (interpretations, insights).

Summary

The language presented and the ideas (information) presented must be correctly attributed to their source(s). I tell my students to opt to quote when there is power and eloquence in the prose. Criticism is more easily paraphrased. Primary sources should be more amply quoted, as long as there is justification—that is, as long as the student writer has something important to say about the quote or about the book as a whole through use of quotes. Look to scholarly essays for examples of what I am advising here. As writers, as researchers, as literary critics, we want to spend more time on the primary sources than on secondary ones (they offer, after all, secondhand information). This needs to be emphasized to students as well. In literary analysis papers, we quote the literature itself to ground the readers of our essays in the primary sources and to help them understand how we interpret these works.

In identifying both source of language and source of information plagiarism in student papers, we need to recognize that these students are avoiding engagement and responsibility. They are in copy mode, which requires little thought. These appropriations of language and ideas and structure and organization are symptoms of larger issues—of tuning out, lack of confidence, lack of comprehension, and lethargy.

Students must learn that there are several approaches to the incorporation of text material, both primary and secondary source material. They can quote, paraphrase, summarize: empower them with these options and give them the rationale behind the choices, so that they are not haphazardly landing on one form of integration—most commonly, that of quoting the source. They need to ask themselves the following questions: When does it make sense to paraphrase or to summarize? Should I quote this entire passage or just a part of it? Will this quote have impact or will it merely serve as filler? I cover these forms of integration in Chapter 5, considering the reason behind the choice.

Reading examples of literary criticism closely will help students to see how the published critics organize academic arguments. Have them look quantitatively at the number of primary source quotes versus secondary source quotes used by the scholar. How much of the material is original? They should be able to identify the scholar's own insights. What kind of balancing act has the scholar accomplished? Whose voice is the dominant voice in the critical article? What forms has source integration taken? Have students examine one quote, one paraphrase, and one summary and determine the reason for the form selected by the critic. Give them concrete examples of fine critical writing. Show them—don't tell them!

Students must evaluate secondary sources to make educated decisions about source integration. Paraphrasing cannot take place without understanding. If they are having difficulty with the jargon used by a specialist, they should be made aware of specialized dictionaries, available in most college library reference centers. Teachers should conference with students who are having difficulty understanding secondary source material.

Something we must also consider—are we, as teachers, referencing our own sources of information and language when we lecture on a work of literature? Pat Fuge, my colleague at West Milford High School in New Jersey, points out (at faculty meetings on the topic of student plagiarism) that we must reference the sources we use in our lectures and class discussions. Clearly, we are role models for our students. We must make the distinction between our own ideas about *Hamlet* and those of the established critics and between our own language and the exact language of the critic. We need to name the specific critics, if we are using their ideas in our discussions.

Through a definition of type, plagiarism will be better understood and accountability will be more readily accomplished because ignorance will no longer be an excuse. Define your terms; give them the background; give them examples. Your students will begin to discover their own voices and their roles in the world of research.

Strategies for Avoiding Plagiarism

We do not always recognize that the topics we assign students may invite plagiarism. Vague assignments that call for the evaluation of literature make it easy for students to plagiarize the ideas of others. Students consult online sources, which give overviews of characterization, plot, and theme, and they hastily patch these elements together in a poorly synthesized essay. It is harder to document plagiarism in these cases because an underlying message is an underlying message—did the student truly evaluate the primary source and determine the theme on his or her own, or did he or she run to SparkNotes and have it readily identified? General assignments such as analyze *Hamlet* in four to five typewritten pages are open invitations to plagiarism for a certain type of student. This is partly because these students may flounder for a point of entry into the text and partly because they do not understand what is required (considering such a vague topic, I certainly empathize) and partly because it is easier not to think too much about the literature—or, perhaps, because they did not read the primary text to begin with. So assignments that call for a focus on characterization, plot, or theme in vague terms are going to produce a large number of responses that include some form of plagiarism—whether it is just lifting a theme from an online source (these students will gather evidence on their own from the primary source) or copying the pattern of claim and evidence directly from the site. Students may plagiarize language, or information, or a combination of both. All of these possibilities are time-consuming for the instructor to check.

As instructors, what we can do to thwart students' attempts at submitting forged papers is to give them precise topics. If we ask for a general book report, we set them up for the retelling of plot in tedious fashion. These "rehashers of text" may not even consult an online source; they will just relentlessly retell the primary text. Many teachers see the book report assignment as a form of documentation, proving that the student read the assigned text. Students pick up on this cue: to them, proof means restating, covering the plot sequence of events. They do not offer insights, for they do not think this is required of them. If this is the case, then we, as teachers, need to clarify what we want from our students. Retelling the story is not acceptable. One paragraph of opinion in the conclusion (which generally takes the form of a vague recommendation—"good summer reading") is not sufficient if our aim is to develop critical thinkers. The book report is a dubious assignment if all that is accomplished is a retelling of storyline. Teach students to write critical papers from the beginning; get them out of copy mode. If we can begin to do this, we can lay the foundation for higher-level thinking in writing and in reading.

If we ask for the theme of a literary work in a book report, then we are likely to get some use of online sources for ideas, because if students have not determined the underlying message on their own, they realize that others before them have. We get a generalized essay on theme, vaguely connected to primary source. It will stay vague and largely topical because student writers do not need to think; the thinking has been done for them.

Consider the following—if you generate a precise topic for students, it will be harder for them to plagiarize a response. Select a more obscure approach; consider topics more cross-curricular in nature—connecting history to literature, science to literature, art to literature, or music to literature (if content permits these connections).

If we sidestep the general analysis accomplished in online study guides that students typically use, and if we avoid asking for plot analysis, theme analysis, and character analysis in such general ways, we are more likely to get genuine work. It may take more time to come up with topics, but in the end it will save us vast amounts of time checking countless papers for instances of cheating. Some of my topics are so offbeat that I have begun calling them my "2 a.m. topics" (consider the desire to escape the confines of existence—through death, through illusion, through distractions provided by the physical world, and through a purging of one's own soul—as explored in any of the texts we have studied this year; consider the role of destruction and the force of creation as they are revealed in the film *Barton Fink*; explore the lure of the forbidden in Roy's *The God of Small Things*), quirky topics that suddenly occur to me in the wee hours of the morning and that, upon further reflection, become viable approaches to the text.

Selecting a quote for students to respond to in generating an all-encompassing thesis is another approach. Instead of leaving the literature wide open so that students always find themselves moving from the general to the specific, let us consider directing them to move from the specific to the more open response: from analysis to synthesis rather than from synthesis to analysis. Incidentally, most essay introductions move from general to specific, which becomes a very tedious, very predictable organization. Let students open up the text from the insight generated by studying a particular quote (selected for its reverberation of theme).

Here are some recommendations for generating more specific topic ideas.

Assignments Using Primary Sources Only

The Close Reading

One of my colleagues at West Milford High School in New Jersey, Eric Nitkinas, assigns close readings of texts as one way of averting plagiarism in student essays. This is an effective assignment as it requires the use of precise literary terms and a methodical approach to literary analysis. A close reading is a line-by-line analysis of a passage of literature chosen for its resonance of theme, the presence of identifiable literary devices, its precise diction, and its original style.

In a close reading, students connect the selected passage to the larger idea of theme—how a particular section of text contributes to the underlying meaning (context). Students do a close analysis and a broad synthesis, including connection (a subtle comparison/contrast, a piece against its backdrop). These approaches call for highly sophisticated analyses and are less likely to invite plagiarism. I select passages for analysis to avoid having students choose the most highly quoted, well-known passages of text (of *Hamlet*, for example), which may be referenced in an online study guide and may give them some ideas to appropriate. Consider selecting more obscure passages, but choose passages that lend themselves to direct connection with theme. If you are afraid of students working together behind the scenes (students appropriating material from other students), then assign a separate passage to each student. This initially time-consuming process will save you time later because you will not have to check for students sharing information and ideas. It will also be less tedious to grade because of the variety of passages and responses. If you wish to assign this as class work, you can select individual passages for close readings in groups. A presentation, rather than a paper, can be generated. This is a skills-oriented assignment in terms of analysis (close reading) and synthesis of literature.

Close reading requires a solid knowledge of literary and poetic devices; students need to learn the jargon and how to apply it. They will be forced to forge connections between device and meaning, to consider how device renders meaning. In this breaking down that is analysis, they will be separating layers of meaning for later unification in a paper. They will synthesize the elements of close analysis—diction, sentence structure, literary devices, poetic devices (sound, visual, olfactory, and tactile)—into a coherent whole and hold it up against the structure that is the novel, play, or poem itself.

You may get some outstanding papers from this assignment, and you may get a number of very weak attempts. Nevertheless, you are likely to get authentic writing that will allow you to target your instruction in device, writing, analysis, and synthesis. You will have very little checking up to do on the integrity of student-generated essays.

Close reading will also be required of students in college literature courses, so this is a nice way to prepare them for future assignments.

The Comparison/Contrast Essay

This particular rhetorical strategy can be extremely useful to teachers, whether students take on a whole subject by whole subject approach to organization (which can include blocking out similarities as one subject and differences as another) or a point-by-point approach to organization. This type of essay is challenging to plagiarize in terms of both content and organization, as it requires knowledge of two subjects and the ability to discern connections and distinctions between them. Using *Hamlet,* for example, students could (quite obviously) compare Hamlet to his foil, Laertes (or Fortinbras)—this has been widely covered in criticism, particularly in online study guides. Less obvious (to students) would be the assigned focus of a comparison/contrast of Hamlet with Ophelia, whose action to his inaction makes her a marvelous choice: her madness in comparison/contrast to his, her overt reaction to her father's murder to his covert reaction to his father's murder, their understandings of filial obligation. The less obvious the approach, the more challenging the composition—students will be forced to think, rather than have others think for them. Character evolution also offers material for a comparison/contrast essay—have them compare/contrast Hamlet at the beginning of the play with Hamlet at the ending of the play.

Clearly, you can also go outside of the text and have students compare/contrast the characters of *Hamlet* (you can select which characters, or have them make selections) with the characters of other Shakespearean texts. Encourage students to pick the less obvious characters or to consider highlighting differences rather than similarities (compare/contrast Richard III with Hamlet, for example). You need not limit students to works by the same author. I have had students compare/contrast Poe's Roderick Usher with Shakespeare's Hamlet. Roderick is entrapped by his obligation to family, as is Hamlet. Both characters court self-destruction. In an obscure topic such as this, I try to give students direction: self-entrapment, self-destruction, family corruption, madness. I have also had students compare/contrast Sethe from Morrison's *Beloved* with Roderick from Poe's "The Fall of the House of Usher," or the character Beloved with the character Madeline: both characters refuse to stay buried, and any male attempt to relegate them to the afterlife (Paul D's, Roderick Usher's) are promptly spurned. Again, here I would be precise and assign a topic with some kind of direction.

These comparison/contrast assignments do not have to focus on character analysis but can be directed to symbols in texts or within a single text, on symbol and its connection to theme. Consider contemporary events in connection to literature with novels that chronicle the human condition: *The Stranger* with contemporary stances on capital punishment, *The Crucible* with contemporary witch hunts. We often explore historical context of the literature, but let us also consider contemporary frameworks, which make literary texts more relevant for students.

Have students compare artwork with literature (the works need not be contemporaneous)—compare/contrast Munch's *The Scream* with Camus's *The Stranger*, or with Hesse's *Steppenwolf*. The underlying messages of these texts are certainly connected. Look at existentialism in art and literature. Compare film and literature, but do not always compare the film version of the text with the text itself. I have had students compare the Coen Brothers' film *Barton Fink* with Joyce's *A Portrait of the Artist as a Young Man*. The final scene of the film is an allusion to Stephen Dedalus's epiphany (Joyce 171).

Students can examine the historical, social, and symbolic backdrop against a character who is indeed a product of that environment. Historical context as a broad framework through which to construct a more precise study of literature is commonly used to generate topics. Consider symbolic backdrop as well—look at Poe's Madeline Usher against the symbolic environment of the house (this is classically done with Roderick Usher).

The less obvious is sometimes the less doable; however, we are not asking students to resolve all issues, all conflicts that arise in analysis, but only to recognize them. We are asking students to engage in the process, to attempt to forge links, and to reach conclusions. This can be accomplished in a comparison/contrast essay. When students have reached an impasse, we can at least be reassured that they arrived there on their own and have come face to face with the writers in themselves and the writers they are analyzing. It is the recognition of impasse that is their discovery.

The comparison/contrast assignment that most effectively deters plagiarism comes from the creative selection of subjects—the less obvious choices. This means that we, as teachers, are constantly on the lookout for material to be compared/contrasted with the literature we cover in our classes.

The Less Predictable Sequence of Points

The unconventional organization (the one that breaks free of storyline in structure) is the preferable one, or it should be. Essays that have other organizing principles are really not unconventional; they may be unconventional in a pile of student–generated essays, but in the real world of critical writing, they are not. Assign an essay in which the absolute requirement is that it cannot follow storyline. This will obviously discourage plot summary—retelling—and, instead, encourage analysis: it is an effective way of obstructing plagiarism. You may ask students to select a symbol from the literature as an organizing principle. In this assignment, students will be required to relate other elements of the novel or play to the symbol and, ultimately, to an underlying message in the text. The symbol becomes the hub of the wheel. The essay's form will be more circular, instead of a linear plot summary. An example would be to select the tarn in Poe's "The Fall of the House of Usher" as a symbol of the dream state (illusion) and to connect the characters, the other images, and the theme to this symbol.

The Synthesis Essay

The pulling together of several subjects in the quest for a thread of connection is another approach that makes plagiarizing harder to accomplish. Have students link separate texts to generate their own connections among works. They will also be noting distinctions. I have had students connect O'Brien's *The Things They Carried* to Oliver Stone's *Platoon* and to a personal interview with a Vietnam veteran (Patrick Loughman, in my particular experience with this topic, who graciously gave of his time to my classes). Although in this assignment students used two fictional sources and one nonfictional source, I required them to synthesize a common experience of the Vietnam War—what did the sources say about the atrocities of war, human brutality, the "brotherhood of soldiers," selfishness and survival, escapism, obligation, patriotism, internal and external conflict? The list is an endless one. This topic seemed impossible for students to plagiarize because it was broad, extensive in nature, and they knew they would not find connections made for them in any online study guide. They knew Mr. Loughman would not be compared to Lieutenant Jimmy Cross (*The Things They Carried*) in an online study guide, so they did not bother to look. They resigned themselves to making their own connections and distinctions. In this case, it was the path of least resistance. Why waste time online if it would not help them directly with the assignment?

You can have students synthesize several short stories by one author, or they might synthesize a poem with a painting and a sculpture. Certainly all collected works—compact discs (individual albums), chapbooks of poetry, collections of short stories, the clothing line of a particular designer, artistic periods of painters—all of these offer subjects for synthesis papers.

The Non Sequitur Approach

In the non sequitur approach you are asking for the printed versions of the online study guides (PinkMonkey, SparkNotes, etc.) to be turned in along with students' essays; that is, you are asking them to turn in potential cheat sheets—material you asked them not to consult. This is the most jarring approach in the prevention of plagiarism. Have students submit printouts of online study guides on the literature they are analyzing in their papers—a bit intimidating, but it works. At the very least, you do not need to review these study guides online, but you can pursue the others not included in student folders.

The Creative Writing Assignment

When it is necessary to document that independent reading, supplementary reading, has been completed—when you need a system for checking up on students' reading, here are some assignments that are less grading intensive because they are not traditional book reports. (I hope to convince you to stop assign-

ing book reports.) These are unconventional approaches in response to reading, which are difficult to plagiarize because they
are so unusual. You are familiar with some of them, I am sure—
the interview format (where students generate interview questions and imagine the author's responses), letters to the author,
newspaper articles—assignments along these lines explore various genres. Some of these, however, also lend themselves to plagiarized sections: ideas from online sources incorporated into
letters or interview responses or articles. I have devised some other
approaches that are somewhat more peculiar, making it more
challenging for students to lift passages to incorporate into their
responses. I encourage you to be creative and develop your own
quirky assignments.

Here are a handful of mine. I have students generate a series
of five haiku (this appeals to them right off the top, because they
know that haiku are short). I have them develop a haiku of symbols for each part of the narrative structure of a novel or play:
five haiku representing the exposition, the rising action, the cli-
max, the falling action, and the denouement. I have also had
them do this same assignment visually (for other learning styles)
through a collage of images. I prefer symbols to actual literal
representations, which are more childish. I require the collage to
have a key for defining symbols in connection to context and for
providing page number references for the selected symbols. I have
them produce a "phrase collage" out of obscure details around
the hub(s) of the theme(s) from the novel. These have to be fairly
obscure details, and page numbers must be included for source
documentation. I have had students create a concrete poem focusing on a minor character and the insights they have into that
character, to be concretized into a symbolic image, rendered
through form and language. You can see that there are endless
possibilities. Here I am emphasizing comprehension—reading over
writing. I do not exclusively assign these unconventional projects.
I tend to do these in connection with independent reading assignments.

With texts we are analyzing collectively in class, I assign traditional academic essays. Objectives are clearly different. In the
unconventional assignment, I am hoping to ensure students have

completely read the literature and have tried to understand it. In a writing assignment, I am teaching both literary analysis skills and communication skills in a traditional form. Some students are competent writers, but poor critics of literature. Others cannot write literary analysis papers effectively, but they are insightful readers of literature. We need to address these separate objectives of teaching analytical reading and essay composition.

Papers Requiring Secondary Source Integration

The Research Assignment

All students must experience the research paper. As mentioned in Chapter 2, I set this up in stages. Many teachers do: they collect notes and working bibliographies prior to accepting the final product, the research paper itself. This does deter plagiarism because we are documenting the process—that students are completing the stages required before synthesis can take place in the final paper. However, there is still room for plagiarism within this process. Students will sometimes turn in index cards generated by a student from a previous year, or they may go through the motions of note-taking because notes are collected as a separate assignment and they need the points, but they may never refer to their notes again: they may just take a paper off an online site before it is due. Passages of the notes may be lifted word for word from a source and not acknowledged by the student with quotation marks. So, even in the preliminary stages, there are opportunities to plagiarize. We know this, which is why we still end up checking a large number of research papers for plagiarism.

Many instructors also require a file folder of sources (usually periodical sources) to be submitted along with the final product. This method is helpful because it makes it convenient for teachers to review sources and serves as a deterrent because students understand that they are turning in their source information with the paper so that it can be checked against their citations and inclusions in text. This is assuming that students have been honest in including all materials. Students are likely to have been honest, however, because they know this teacher will be checking. If used as a preliminary research assignment, to teach research skills, this approach is fine, but remember that it is artificial in terms of an authentic research experience.

It is as artificial an experience as assigning a certain number of periodical sources, circulating texts, or reference works to be used in writing the research paper, as though a magic formula of necessary sources could be determined. We cannot possibly know all that is out there on the subjects students are researching. It is falsely prophetic of us to itemize number and type of sources. In numbering the amounts and in listing the types of sources required, we are setting up an inauthentic research experience. It is the students' job to uncover as much information as possible using the resources available to them: maybe interviewing a writer would be appropriate; maybe a television documentary would be appropriate; maybe a reference work or a circulating text would be appropriate.

If a bibliography is done properly, then we do have the means to check a variety of sources for suspected passages. It requires more effort than scanning a submitted folder of sources, but the submission of a paper without hard copies of source material is a more realistic research experience for students.

THE STAGES OF RESEARCH: A DIFFERENT SORT OF PROGRESSION

My approach is a different sort of progression (see Chapter 2). I do not move from working bibliography to notes to rough draft to final copy. I move from freewriting (which I collect) to literary analysis essay (in response to primary sources) to form (model for research) to term paper (integration of secondary sources). When I do finally reach the stage of assigning the term paper, I do monitor preliminary stages, but I emphasize freewriting over note-taking. I emphasize student ideas over source ideas. This does not mean that I do not teach them to value factual information or to value the ideas of the experts. It means, however, that I highlight their responses to content: the subjective over the objective—how they process facts or ideas more than how they accumulate and organize this information. Thinking is emphasized over rote transference of information.

Freewriting in Depth

Students are assigned a play or novel (or can choose a selection from a list of titles) to read and respond to in freewriting. They must generate a minimum of ten pages of freewriting by the time they have completed the novel or play. Their freewriting is not a collection of detailed notes on the novel or play. It includes personal reaction, outlandish connections, risk-taking interpretations of text. It is whatever occurs to them as they are reading the novel. The only approach I will not accept in their freewriting is the rehashing of text. Teach them to break free of narrative chronology. Teach them to have their own organizing principles by having them move away from the structure of the play or novel. I allow them to fixate on symbols, characters, images, literary devices, impressions, resonating quotes, sentence structure, diction, their opinions, complaints about level of difficulty or writer's style—how Roderick Usher reminds them of a close relative. Personal responses are valid because, through them, the work comes alive for the student. Although personal connections are not conventionally acceptable for inclusion in students' formal writing, they have served the purpose of making the reading meaningful in some way that impacts comprehension and will translate into more energetic academic writing in the next stage of the process. The literature has become three dimensional because students have provided that third dimension. Ultimately, we are hoping that within ten pages, somewhere tucked away in the margin or in a partial phrase, is the *beginning of a thesis idea*.

This freewriting will be collected along with the final product, the term paper. It will allow me to document the progression of students' ideas, to see their ideas firsthand—how sophisticated or topical they are. Because students know this writing is free form, they are less likely to plagiarize: they see informal writing as less valuable (though it is immensely more valuable) than formal writing, and they understand that almost anything goes (except retelling of plot) in this form. They are less uptight writing in this manner and less likely to consult the "experts," the online study guides.

Content (critical thinking) is emphasized over grammatical correctness and style. As Natalie Goldberg advises writers in a list of rules in her text *Writing Down the Bones*, "*Don't cross out. (That is editing as you write. Even if you write something you didn't mean to write, leave it)*" (8). She explains it like this:

> First thoughts have tremendous energy. It is the way the mind first flashes on something. The internal censor usually squelches them, so we live in the realm of second and third thoughts, thoughts on thought, twice and three times removed from the direct connection of the first fresh flash. (Goldberg 9)

Goldberg is writing here about the creative process, not the academic writing process, not the research project. But what she advises can be applied to the research experience because, in evaluating the external, the writers' own thoughts are being pulled out of themselves, their reaction to the world, and their responses to it. Researching thoughts is also part of the research process: it should be, certainly. Unfortunately, some student writers are, as Goldberg describes, "liv[ing] in the realm of second and third thoughts," (9) in the secondhand sources they consult. Nothing, then, comes from them.

Elbow's classic text on freewriting, *Writing with Power*, offers many approaches to freewriting that can be adapted both to writer and to topic: "The Open-ended Writing Process," and "The Loop Writing Process" are two chapters in his book that speak to more precise uses of freewriting. Here are some particularly marvelous recommendations for fine-tuning what he calls "The Open-ended Writing Process:"

> first, let yourself start without knowing where you are going and even get more lost as you proceed; and second, alternate between nonstop writing and pausing to focus on what you've written. As long as your nonstop writing is going well there is no need, of course, to stop and focus. But if you are writing and writing without getting anywhere, it will help to move deliberately back and forth between immersion and perspective. Doing so will help each wave of writing carry you farther and make each pause not just a rest but an occasion for progress. (Elbow 56)

Students should be encouraged to explore their own ideas, even preconceived notions, about a topic before they proceed to the stage of finding sources. This is the beginning of dialogue, a speaking back to the sources, a constant reassessing of the interpretive position, as evidence and the ideas of others enter the conversation. Elbow's advice encourages writers to get lost, which is a discovering of ideas previously unknown. The newness of these ideas can surprise even the authors. Also, Elbow's recommendation is to stop to take a breath, to take in a landscape, to have a kind of aerial view of the freewriting "perspective," as the freewriting is starting to engrave its own topography. For me, the process is metaphorically described by Poe in "The Fall of the House of Usher:"

> While the objects around me—while the carvings of the ceilings, the somber tapestries of the walls, the ebon blackness of the floors, and the phantasmagoric armorial trophies which rattled as I strode, were but matters to which or to such as which, I had been accustomed from my infancy—while I hesitated not to acknowledge how familiar was all this—I still wondered to find how unfamiliar were the fancies which ordinary images were stirring up. (258)

This is as good as any possible description of the freewriting process: moving past the familiar ideas to the unfamiliar ideas, to less mundane understandings.

ILLUSTRATIONS: SAMPLES OF STUDENTS' FREEWRITING

What follows are several examples from my high school students' freewriting (some weak, some strong) in response to Arundhati Roy's *The God of Small Things*. I have selected brief passages from students' complete entries (length requirement: two typewritten, double-spaced pages per chapter). Note that freewriting is forgiving of grammatical and mechanical mistakes; critical thinking is emphasized, and form is abandoned.

In my selection, I begin with two examples of poor freewriting and move toward examples of outstanding freewriting to illustrate and define freewriting—the fertile ground of original thinking.

> Throughout this chapter [Chapter 2] they are trying to tell the story of when they picked up Margeret and Sophie but tell so many side stories in between. We learn that Pappachi discovered

a rare species of moth but does not get recognized for it because he retired. He grows angry and takes it out on his wife, Mammachi. He beat her for being beautiful and when Chacko sees it one day, he yells at his father. Pappachi never talked to his wife again.

This student has summarized plot, rather than analyzing text. Clearly, this is an example of weak freewriting: this retelling is not what we want students to be doing in their freewriting. Students are in the habit of rehashing; essentially, they are poorly paraphrasing exquisite writing (what a waste of time and energy). They do this largely so that they can copy rather than think, but also because they feel compelled to prove to the teacher that they read the assigned reading. Hold them accountable for analyzing it beyond merely reading it! This student writer is not engaged in a dialogue with the primary source. There are also some misunderstandings or oversimplifications of text in this passage. I am more forgiving of misunderstandings than I am of rehash. This student needs to be encouraged to engage the text and to offer interpretations of the text. There is, perhaps, one slight attempt made at offering insight, "He beat her for being beautiful." This is somewhat incorrect, but at the same time there is some innate truth to the statement, and I would advise the student to begin freewriting on this chapter again, in an attempt to explore the essential truth of her assertion.

Here is another example of plot summary—weak freewriting:

The third chapter opens in the present and the Ayanenem house is filthy with dead insects everywhere. Baby Kochamma only cares about the television. She speaks about a Donahue show on television and you realize how horrible Baby Kochammas life really is and you see how ugly and unpleasant she is. Estha refuses to talk to anyone and is extremely reserved, he is obsessed with cleanliness.

Although this is somewhat of an improvement over the first example, because there are some interpretations (but nothing striking or original), it is still largely plot summary: the student does not attempt to understand any underlying significance in character behavior, setting description, or character description. There is no analysis and certainly no synthesis, no connections made to material read in previous chapters. This is not productive free-writing—from which a thesis idea might eventually emerge. This is barren freewriting.

Against these examples of weak informal writing, I offer you better examples of what freewriting should accomplish. This is a student response to Chapter 1 of Roy's novel:

> Rahel is a very artistic girl and she tries to make everything beau-tiful. We see an example of this when she decorates the cow dung. She is trieing to make something ugly beautiful and with good intention [intention] she gets into trouble by the nouns [nuns]. She looks at the world in a strange way, in an artistic way, and no one can understand this. She is truly unique and different and does not care what anyone thinks.

This somewhat repetitive entry shows the student is trying to work out a detail, one that might initially strike a student as an unpleasant or offensive detail. She takes this initial risk in focus-ing in on an unusual description in the novel. This student is certainly not recopying as filler for an entry: she is attempting to work out the meaning of a description in connection to the char-acter and trying to understand the underlying significance of both the character and the action. This is more productive freewriting than offered in the previous two examples. There is a slight tem-plate of argument embedded in this entry, a balance of detail and interpretation that makes the entry more formal (more like an essay) than we really want to see in freewriting. I say this because this form (which student writers are so used to) can negatively impact their freewriting. Though better than the predictable re-telling that removes ownership of ideas, the predictable writing pattern (argument) sets parameters on original ideas. The con-ventional organization of detail and interpretation, which is ex-pected in formal academic essays, should be avoided in freewriting, which should be without form, without shape, with-out boundaries. Boundaries limit ideas and confine associations; they do not let students explore all the possibilities. Freewriting should be meandering, not organized in predictable academic patterns.

Here is another student's productive freewriting; this one is written in response to Chapter 2 of *The God of Small Things*:

> Another symbol I have found is in Rahel's watch. It says that her toy watch always say ten to two, but she wishes for a watch which she can adjust the time. I think this is foreshadowing how she wishes she could change time, and go back in time, and how her life changes so drastically so soon, and if she could just go back in time, she could change it. Also it mentions her glasses in which she sees red, which foreshadows her life after Velutha maybe? I might be reading into that too much . . . .

Clearly, you can see the student above is trying to determine underlying significance of a detail in the text, of an object on which Roy has lingered and that the student, therefore, recognizes as important. The student attempts to explain its significance as a symbol. She synthesizes the text as well, bringing forward what she has already read and projecting ahead into what she may encounter later in the book. Notice that the writing is more meandering in form; she leaps from one idea to the next. This partial entry is more energetic because form is not confining her. Though there is still some tentativeness, she is not afraid to be wrong—this is important. We need to help students have the courage to take interpretive risks. In later stages, if their claims are incorrect they will not find evidence to support them from the primary source. That is fine. Some claims need to be abandoned because they are inaccurate or because there is insufficient evidence to support them in the formal writing stage. All ideas are tentative in freewriting; this allows the student freedom to consider all possibilities. Note that all quotes should be in quotation marks, as they would be in notes.

Here is another fine example from the same student and from the same entry (a response to Chapter 2 of Roy's novel):

> "Et tu, Brute?" This is a famous story of betrayal. Ammu tells the twins that they can't trust anyone. I'm pretty sure this is before Velutha dies, but Estha still says, "'*Et tu, Brute?*—Then fall Ceaser!'" and he falls. I believe that this is significant because he betrays Velutha in a sense when he says that Velutha hurt him to the officer, and that he was guilty. Then Estha falls, parallel with his life declining afterwards.

Although there is some naïveté exhibited here, there is also the determination to understand beyond what is merely topical. The student is picking up on diction and its meaning on two levels: "falling" becomes "declining"; that is, she articulates the connection between the character's action and his metaphorical fall from grace. She is synthesizing without being fully conscious of doing so. Her mind is making connections that she has yet to fully articulate, but ideas are brewing, and the process is very exciting. In the formal writing stage she can articulate these ideas, forge the connections more lucidly for the reader. Here she encloses direct language in quotation marks because she recognizes that with full sentences of direct extraction, she must—though she did not recognize, in the previous sample of freewriting, that partial quotes should be enclosed within quotation marks as well. In addition, the exact location of quotes, page numbers, should have been provided.

Next is an example of a more emotional reading of text that has a more intimate tone and a sympathetic eye. This student demonstrates he is fully engaged in the novel. Here is a part of his entry in response to Chapter 6 of Roy's novel:

> After anticipating this day for a while, the actors get set on their stage. Rahel and Estha see this whole *"What will Sophie Mol Think?"* as a play that has been practiced over and over again. You feel their emotions all separately, Chacko's excitement, Rahel and Estha's need to hide. And after all this, we find out Sophie Mol is normal (Selfish, bratty, playful) kid. This introduction of her makes us want to like her, she is a joker. We also tend to look at how adorable Rahel and Estha are, and how they want to most likely ruin this well-scripted act (with Rahel hiding behind the curtain and Estha not having a "How d'you do?" in him). You feel a little bad for Chacko when he introduces "My wife, Margaret." When you read that line, you almost feel embarrassed for him [. . .] It seems as if Margaret has scripted her [Sophie Mol] as much as they [Baby Kochamma, Ammu] did with Rahel and Estha. "We've come here to recover from the shock." That's not something a kid under 10 would say.

Overlooking, as we should in any assessment of freewriting, the comma splices, quirky capitalization (interestingly, this is something Roy uses stylistically, which he may unconsciously be mimicking), what we observe here is an open-mindedness in the above freewriting response and an attempt to be sympathetic to characters' humanity, a deep reading with some emotional layering that is certainly more welcome than a dry restating of the sequence of events. This student perceived the dynamics in the relationships among these characters. He picked up Roy's more subtle clues, and his writing demonstrates an engagement with text but also with self. Most of this will not make its way into the student's formal writing, but what he has pulled out of himself is an enhanced understanding of characterization that will serve him well when he formalizes his ideas about the novel. He will have this to draw on—he has understood the facade of character—projected and protected identities. And there is layering here—one can have a marvelous discussion with this student about mask in fiction. (Again, the student should have provided page numbers for direct quotes included in his freewriting.)

What follows are several sophisticated entries by another student in response to various chapters (as indicated) of Roy's novel. The first entry is written in response to Chapter 1:

> I do not understand why the family is mad at Estha. It seems that he had something to do with Sophie Mol's buried fate. There are many life/death themes. In the beginning there's an image of a fly hitting a window. Most of the imagery is jarring, industrialization/nature, religion/popculture, the two gods ["Big God", "Small God"], and Rahel and Estha. The only real similarity between them is that they are both soft spoken. It's interesting that Baby Kochamma distrusts Rahel more than Estha. Perhaps they are responsible for seperate sins. It's interesting how Baby Kochamma joined a convent, completely unselfish feat, yet gives herself an alias of a diamond, something selfish and materialistic. This is a turning point foreshadowing her superficial behavior later in life. There are also plenty of child images associated to her old age.

This student is not afraid to admit confusion about a character; this is a positive use of freewriting. The student will pay attention, awaiting the explanation. He conjectures—"perhaps"—and attempts to connect, to synthesize detail with theme. This student notes contradictions, complexities (so crucial to writing the "A" academic essay, which never offers oversimplification but embraces ambiguity in literature as irresolvable) and is not afraid of intellectual risks. This is highly productive freewriting. It is also correct freewriting in that it is truly stream of consciousness in its movement and in its associations. You can see the inherent logic in flow, but there are also non sequiturs. The student can surely mine this freewriting to unearth points when he is ready to formalize his ideas in an essay. He has ideas that he will probably encounter in criticism later on, written in more sophisticated language. However, the ideas here are original: you can see how one idea tumbles out of another.

Here is another example from the same student, when he takes on imagery in analyzing Chapter 10 of Roy's novel:

> Ammu is associated with a tranquil blue, which is odd since she is a wild spirit. But, the river is also compared to this character, being said that it appears calm but it is reckless deep within. The insect imagery is confusing, ants follow each other like a mindless army or communists, moth's float around without harming anyone, like dreams, and wasps are more vicious beings, associated with yellow and Sophie Mol. Estha and Rahel's secret of becoming communists is sealed in a pickle jar, meaning it's a family secret, and it is a red color, like the communist color. Velutha's father and brother are seen in pairs, furthering the double imagery. All of the double imagery, Estha and Rahel, the gods ["Big God", "Small God"], are also seen as one.

The student moves from color imagery to double imagery in a somewhat unpredictable flow, but this is true freewriting, freely following the ideas as they originate. This would not be acceptable in terms of organization (because it is without transition) in formal writing, but it makes for wonderfully productive freewriting. The student did not stop to forge a transition (and possibly lose the next idea as it occurred to him: double imagery). Form is not required; in fact, it is to be avoided at this stage as it is limiting. Without form the student was able to land on another separate idea that is not necessarily connected to the previous one. Form will come into being in the process. The student can later decide between two possible focal points (thesis ideas) for a critical essay on Roy's novel: color imagery or double imagery as it connects to theme. Again, the writer does not merely assemble the evidence of literary devices but connects these devices to meaning. Although he has offered interpretations in connection to color, he must synthesize this pattern and connect it to underlying theme. This decision of focal points can be based on what intrigues the student more, or on the evidence the student can muster at a later stage. If the student can link the two, color imagery and double imagery in an all-encompassing thesis, then he does not need to give up either idea. Clearly both color and double images create contrast, foils, shades. If the student starts to explore this in depth, he might be able to articulate a thesis that merges the two ideas.

Here is a final example from this student—from his best entry. This is based on Chapter 19 of *The God of Small Things*:

> The fairy tale imagery is indeed strongest in this chapter. The most ironic usage is Baby Kochamma being "a fairy godmother." She helps the children out of a possible prison sentence but she does it for greed. What's really funny is that Estha and Rahel listen to Baby Kochamma's fabrication of Velutha like they are being told a story, or a fairy tale. There was also some food imagery "Caked with mud. Drenched in Coca-Cola," all sugary products best suited for children. The paperweight with the dancers seem to be symbolic towards Velutha and Ammu's relationship, trapped and confined. It was also described as being underwater, like Sophie Mol's fate.

This entry offers a sense of emerging framework for a possible analysis of the novel—a myth or fairytale—with a movement from detail to detail. It manages to remain unconfined, even as thread is linking one idea to the next. Form can be seen drifting over the surface and operating as an undercurrent in this writing. Again, direct extractions of language should have parenthetical page tags.

Occasionally, I have requested that prior to submitting their freewriting, students use a highlight marker to trace the progression of their ideas to the thesis idea, to follow train of thought in their freewriting. This documents how the thesis idea (the original thesis idea) evolved in the process of freewriting.

RHETORICAL DEVICES: THE SEARCH FOR FORM IN INFORMAL WRITING

Freewriting relies on chaos and contradiction in a space where ideas move in many directions seeking expression, getting tangled up in each other, merging and redefining each other. Formal writing has some relationship to design. It has an organizing principle. But organization is not a static symmetry of evidence and interpretation, because form itself has an inherent instability: it is a negotiation, and its movement is one of give and take. Chaos and design exist in delicate imbalance. Spellmeyer, in his book *Common Ground*, explains the nature of form in composition:

> Whereas conventional pedagogy equates the achievement of co-herent "form" with the elimination of complexity, form is instead, as Paul de Man observes, the record of complexity, the record of an "endless" and revealing "interplay" between the voices within a dia-logue. Form does not precede the act of composing, but emerges from tensions between the voice of experience and the voice of convention, between the writer's conflicting impulses and her desire to achieve an expressive unity: form is, more simply, "a process on the way to completion." (55)

Freewriting allows the student to participate in amorphous writing as part of the initial process of composition. Form is not imposed, then, at the outset, but is allowed to come into being.

In teaching students to write, I do model form through example. I introduce students to a variety of rhetorical strategies. I do this so that they have some sense of the possibilities of how content finds a form. These forms are not to serve as overlays upon student ideas that originate in freewriting, but they are to be seen as literal demonstrations of ideas taking shape in the writings of others. A teacher can use an anthology of published essays to provide models of rhetorical devices.

I begin by distinguishing between analysis (a looking at the parts) and synthesis (a looking at the whole). Analysis includes process analysis and comparison/contrast. Synthesis includes cause and effect, narration, and description. One can argue that all types can be simultaneously regarded as analysis and synthesis: one cannot break down though analysis without reassembling, for coherency's sake, through synthesis. But if considered as a particular kind of breaking down (achieved through looking at similarities and differences in comparison/contrast), it is clearly a way of dissecting a subject to better understand it. Process analysis requires the breaking down through a series or levels of understanding—the steps of a process. Writers synthesize these methods of breaking down, linking the two halves of the paper in a comparison/contrast essay and forging an understanding of process through an organization in a series of logically placed steps. Writers pull it all together under an all-encompassing thesis idea.

Cause and effect, narration, and description are ways of synthesizing content because they are processes that ultimately unify. Synthesis is a looking at the whole picture or whole story, or moving forward to the whole explanation. Cause and effect requires linkage (the factors and the consequences), narration threads time, and description unifies observation. Analysis is also obviously involved in these strategies: in order to label causes and effects of an event, one must break down the discrete units of time, the details of a subject.

In refining a topic, students must consider what they hope to learn about the topic; they should be required to talk about what they really want to find out about the topic in a paper. For example, if the essay is on World War I, is the student going to focus on a particular battle, general, front? Does the student know for certain that he or she does not want to explore the aftermath of the Great War? Narrowing down the topic, defining the parameters, helps the student to focus on what the paper will cover.

FORMALIZING THE PROCESS OF INCORPORATING SECONDARY SOURCES

The parameters set by the students should be well defined. In general, with respect to the topic, students should think of the narrowing-down process by imagining that they are contributing a chapter-length piece to a textbook on the subject: the scope of student papers should be only that wide. If their topic is the Vietnam War, they can obviously find volumes of information on a library shelf. They need to think in terms of refinement: one focus that is a contribution to an understanding of the subject area, a very narrow part of the whole. In Boyer and Nissenbaum's *Salem Possessed*, the chapter "Witchcraft and Social Identity" is a good model for scope (the title suggests its particular focus): a student research paper should be that well defined in terms of parameters. Papers that are too wide are overview papers only and contribute little to students' understanding of the subject. There is no intimacy with subject in a survey paper. Each chapter in Boyer and Nissenbaum's text has an organizing principle at work (a thesis idea), but the entire text has an evolving thesis at work—the larger task of a book-length work on a subject.

It is also true that in process, the thesis of the research paper will be an evolving one. Students cannot have on blinders—a true researcher is open to all the information accessible on a topic. If it is a controversial topic, students need to be open to both sides of the argument: they must consider opposing claims. Rather than making the information fit their preconceived notions about a subject, they should synthesize the accessible information, both primary and secondary, into an all-inclusive central idea.

The central idea, or thesis, must reflect the students' point of view. It must be subjective. Students must evaluate the information, not just collect it. If students alter their original thinking on a topic based on new information they discover, they should write a process analysis paper (a "journey" paper that takes the readers with the students on their movement from one initial position to a new final position on the topic). This is more honest than pretending to have always viewed the subject in this "new" way. Integrity should be demanded on this point.

A "journey" paper arrives at an interpretive stance that is grounded in several theories or insights into the controversial subject: it is a process analysis (sequence of steps) essay. This paper takes a position with respect to the understandings already out there and defends that position by examining the various claims offered by the experts. It is a journey through other understandings of a subject to arrive at one that satisfies the student writer, the evaluator of the sources. To simply restate the position of the majority, without thinking, is to generate a report, to gather without thinking, to recopy without responding. Forewarn students, when they are writing a position paper on a controversial topic, that midway through the process they may do an about-face, a 180-degree turn, and begin to agree with the side they initially opposed. Should they then simply pretend to have been in agreement with the opposing side all along? There is a dishonesty in this approach, a pretense students themselves recognize. It makes them uncomfortable, as it should.

Advise students to write a process analysis paper, instead of a "new" position paper. Have them write a "journey" paper: encourage them to retrace the steps they took to arrive at this "new" understanding, which is now so far away from the original understanding. How did they come to value the arguments of the opposing side and to see the logic in those arguments? How did the evidence compel them—was it through new evidence alone or through the pointing out of weaknesses by the opposing side that turned them around in their own thinking? Revealing the process that took them to this new place in their understanding of the subject could generate one of the strongest essays these students will ever write. Why? Because in demonstrating how the other side won them over, they will be persuading us, the readers, to follow in their footsteps—to arrive at the same place in a newfound understanding of a subject. The reading audience will see the process of thinking, of exploring, of delving deeply into the arguments of both sides. This will not be a topical essay because the journey will be meaningful: it has involved the writer deeply; it has tested previously held convictions and imploded them. This is what the authentic research experience is about— finding out, yes—but then assessing: this is the opening up of doors and the meandering into rooms within the mind. Ultimately, student writers come face to face with a mirror—they experience recognition, not only of information, but of what they themselves bring to an understanding of content knowledge.

NOTE-TAKING FOR THE RESEARCH PAPER

Once students have consulted all sources, the note-taking process begins. The thesis is still in its formative stages, but there is a sense of direction to the note-taking. In order for note-taking to be meaningful, there must be a focus. Note-taking should take place within this emerging sense of interpretive argument. Students make selections of sources based on a semi-articulated thesis idea. They have scanned tables of contents and indexes. They know, or should know, how the references will be useful. They should be assessing relevance, how the ideas of the expert will exist in the framework they are constructing. They should not make the mistake of thinking that the sources are the framework.

If they do that, they have failed to generate a research paper—
what they are doing instead is writing the report. If they allow
the sources to direct them, the paper will come from someplace
outside themselves. They will be distanced from the subject, more
likely to lose interest in it, and ultimately they will relinquish
ownership of it: it will become someone else's property to which
they sign their names. They will have lost faith in their own ability to think. They will have failed themselves, their teachers, and
the assignment.

Note-taking involves several forms of text incorporation:
quoting, paraphrasing, summarizing, all of which must be meticulously documented both within the notes and within the paper. I advise students to be selective in quoting (to avoid the copy
mode even in the note-taking stage) and to attempt to paraphrase
and summarize more frequently. This will save them time later,
when incorporating sources into the paper. They will not want to
have too many quotes in the paper; they will want to avoid sub-
merging their own voices in their research papers. If they do not
paraphrase and summarize information in their notes, then they
are simply putting off this inevitable task to when they are more
likely pressed for time in the composition of the paper.

The fourth element of note-taking is the most important: the
writing down of original responses to the ideas of the external
sources. This is internalizing the information, testing it simultaneously against other texts on the topic and testing it against
their own hypotheses, against preconceived notions about the
topic. Students need to consider if they are agreeing or disagree-
ing with the information in the articles and books (secondary
sources), based on their own experience with primary sources:
they need to determine if secondary sources challenge, deny, enhance, or support their understandings of primary sources. They
need to consider what ideas are triggered in themselves in response. Through this process, they construct the essay's framework. Students need to consider if they are finding that their
central ideas are evolving in response to the new information.
They should be open to new information. They should not appropriate ideas and present them deceptively as their own, of
course. But they may recognize the impact these new ideas have
on their thesis idea. Students must integrate information from

secondary sources with information from primary sources and must be synthesizing all of this material in the evolution of thesis.

As long as the thesis is a reflection of the student's own insights, it can be considered original. It should reflect a synthesis of information, largely shaped by a response to primary sources.

OUTLINING

Once students have assembled notes, I ask them to generate several outlines to allow them to visualize the spine of the paper. Outlining gives students options for more interesting presentations of ideas. This step may seem in contradiction to earlier discussions of form as an organic process, as design reveals itself through composition. Free writing allows design to arise through informal exploration of ideas. Outlining is a later stage in the progression from freewriting (informal) to formal writing. It is necessary in the composition of research papers because of the amount of material that needs to be organized (primary and secondary sources of information within the matrix of subjective stance).

I do, however, tell my students that once they start writing the first draft they can abandon the outline (it remains a helpful reference because it includes points they initially set out to make) if their instincts take over and the actual composing of the paper moves their ideas and evidence in other ways, ways they could not predict beforehand. Composition is more important than outlining. Outlining is more extrinsic to the process (artificial). Composition is more intrinsic to the process (natural).

Outlining, though, can be a creative stage. This exploring of the possibilities of organization will inject some energy into the synthesis of a body of notes and ideas. The outlines accommodate the focus (thesis) of the paper and the main points of the research paper. In the composition of a lengthy work, outlining (generating several outlines) is extremely helpful in creating a cogent dialogue from a cacophony of voices: it allows the student to experiment with ways of communicating so the voices of the outsiders and the voice of the student writer are heard clearly. It allows students to recognize divergence and relevance. It need not be conventional and detail-oriented. I ask students to outline points only and play with their organization in the outline. If students write an outline overburdened with details, then the outline will not go through the necessary series of drafts to become the organizational strategy it should be. If students later wish to add evidence, once they have committed to a game plan, that is fine. I only require the process, not the final product.

COMPOSITION

After outlining, students can begin to compose the paper. In composition, other stages are fully absorbed, and the act of writing is a confrontation with the totality of newly acquired knowledge, of outside information, but more important, with self.

Students need to understand that their initial ideas about the primary source are valid, and often they will see these ideas legitimized in the criticism they encounter. They can paraphrase, summarize, or quote these critics (citing these sources) to point out that these critics, too, read the primary source in the same way. These encounters in validation enhance their papers and their interpretations and build confidence.

Students should not have blinders on when they do research; that is, they should not look only for information that supports their point of view. Research requires a broad-minded approach. We teach students to be open to the understandings of others; clearly, they will learn from these understandings. In researching a subject, a student's thesis will certainly be impacted by source information. Teachers must emphasize the idea of an evolving thesis. Students cannot ignore the information out there on the topic—if they do, research is meaningless. What they need to do is synthesize the information, both primary and secondary, into a unique point of view. This is strikingly different from the literary analysis paper written in response to the primary source alone. In writing the research paper, however, students absolutely cannot offer a scholar's idea as their thesis. (Clearly, student writers cannot offer an "original" point of view and then cite a source after it; worse, they cannot plagiarize a scholar's idea and present it as their own.) Students have to be engaged in a dialogue with multiple sources of information for this assignment. They are not simply responding to the writer of the literary work, but they are now also responding to historical information, contemporary information, critical articles on the literature, biographical information on the writer, other primary sources, letters the writer wrote to his or her publisher, lover, mother, brother. . . . What disorder. No wonder students panic and plagiarize. Help them to sort through all this, to have their own ideas. This is no easy feat for the teacher, either, but few of us acknowledge this as a daunting task in our presentations of the research process. We fixate, instead, on the mundane tasks—the accumulation of notes and of sources, topic selection, format, documentation style. These, admittedly, cannot be overlooked, but they should not be discussed to the exclusion of the meaning of research itself. Students must be the dominant presence and the filter of all information—sometimes presenting it exactly, in the sources' language, sometimes translating into their own language, sometimes condensing it, sometimes partially incorporating original language, but always, always, always reacting to it—attempting to understand it—processing it (and documenting it).

Summary

Freewriting is the concrete representation of the mind at work. Allow students to engage in dialogue with the primary sources in freewriting and then progress to widening the conversation to include the scholars and experts (in their outlines and in their final papers). If you legitimize the authorship of student writers, validate their right to generate ideas, then you instill in them a desire to have a point of view. Students can find their ways through challenging texts if we acknowledge that there are seemingly endless paths.

The Proper Integration of Sources

Writing a research paper is like dominating a conversation. It is steering a conversation in a direction in which the writer wishes to move.

Source integration is connected to fluency in writing, to the establishment of voice. Many forces impinge on voice, including students' own insecurities. Often, students would rather have others speak for them—others meaning accepted authority figures in a field of research: the scholars, critics, experts. Students need to have confidence in their own analytical abilities, and the byproduct of this confidence is the predominant voice.

Teaching source integration needs to be envisioned as a layering of voices. The overall voice should be that of the student, the least established voice of them all, but the original, authentic voice. This voice should be directed toward engaging the primary source—the novel, play, or poem. Most of the paper should reflect this dynamic: most of the direct quoting should be of primary source material.

Also on the loom are the voices of the secondary sources. These need to be threaded through the fabric, but they should not become the established frame of the paper. The purpose of the secondary sources is to enhance, to expand the central argument of the paper—threads that fill out the original pattern.

Secondary voices contribute to the movement on the page. The student writer must move fluently from the dialogue engaged in with the primary source, outward to incorporate the secondary voices: outward and inward, left and right, forward and backward, synthesizing all voices, but the substance of the paper is the back and forth dialogue with the primary source, the work of literature, the subject of study. It is an exciting, vibrant process: controlling all the voices, layering them correctly, allowing for interruptions in thought, understanding how they fit together, and where they come apart. Nothing need be intimidating in all this; no final resolution may be attainable. It is the suspending of all this chaos that is the acknowledgment of complexities, embracing several ways of understanding. Though argument is linear, the synthesis part of the process of forging argument is not linear. And the analysis part of the process is meandering—the student's own exploration of the subject of study.

Argument ultimately imposes some kind of shape, but it must leave some doors open—a final thought here, a challenge there, unresolved discourse among critics here: it is a loosely tied bow. It is only a sketch; movement comes from what we attach to it. It is not stationary but vibrates with a collection of voices. It moves outward in many directions from points considered.

Students must work on fluidity through use of their own voices. We want them to paraphrase and to summarize more often than we want them to quote. When they quote we want them to use partial quotes more often than full-sentence quotes and certainly more often than lengthy quotes. When inserting lengthy quotes, we want students to be certain they are fully considering their own reactions to them; a balanced (length-wise and quality-wise) response is required. The brittle colon coupled with full-length quote insertion should occur minimally in a paper; it is stilted and stands out as such.

The writing style of the student must be maintained through the paper. This is one of the most important weapons against plagiarism. Students are fashioning an argument in their own words, and though we still may have to battle source of language plagiarism on some fronts (incorrect paraphrasing or summarizing) we are moving in the right direction if students are primarily using their own language.

Forms of incorporation—quoting, paraphrasing, summarizing—should be strategically selected by each student for intended purpose in the paper. Students should move deftly among these choices in the composition of the research essay: knowing when it would be more effective to summarize than to insert a lengthy passage from the source; knowing when paraphrasing is a better choice than quoting.

Boundaries become an important issue in source integration. The boundary between the idea of a critic and that of a student is most important. The parenthetical tag used in MLA format indicates that what preceded it came from that source. If students are responding to the source, in a back and forth dynamic, they need to make clear where their ideas end and the critics' ideas begin—and vice versa as well. If students are using first person, then it will be easier to keep this clear—when they are offering their own ideas (certainly a student may use first person in research writing—as evidenced in critical articles in academic disciplines). If a student is using the more formal third person in an essay, delineating boundaries becomes more difficult.

As an illustration of use of first person in academic writing, here is a portion of Showalter's thesis from her essay "Representing Ophelia: Women, Madness, and the Responsibilities of Feminist Criticism":

> Tracing the iconography of Ophelia in English and French painting, photography, psychiatry, and literature, as well as in theatrical productions, I will be showing first of all the representational bonds between female insanity and female sexuality. Second, I want to demonstrate the two-way transaction between psychiatric theory and cultural representation. (223)

Also note that this list approach to thesis construction is more sophisticated than a typical student list approach: Showalter clearly synthesizes; that is, she completely articulates her idea, noting relationships among the elements of her list. Notice, too, that she uses more than one sentence to state her thesis.

When using third person, the inexperienced student writer finds it a more complex composition process to create boundaries. Here, the "Readability" section of the *MLA Handbook for Writers of Research Papers* should be covered: writers can vary the way they integrate a source using MLA format. They can include the author of the ideas in the sentence construction, and then they need only provide the location (paragraph or page number, depending on whether that source is an Internet source or a print source, if the location information is available) in the parenthetical citation. Here is an example of the source boundary issue from a student writer:

Leonard Freed's black and white photographs have always fasci-
nated me. By viewing his collection, *Leonard Freed: Photographs
1954–1990*, I am taken on a journey, to places I've never been
and people I've never met; I can hear the noises, smell the odors,
as if I was a part of the scene. He portrays people from all over
the world and exhibits meaningful pictures as sad and funny as
life itself; some of these contrasts are presented in an almost hu-
morous way. With ceaseless curiosity and sensitivity, Freed approaches the tragedies and summits of life, zealous to document
the unexpected, the unforeseen, presenting the viewer with
unsought aspects of pain and joy. Although he is a reporter, his
focus is not sensationalist; rather he finds something that none of
us would ever discover, and what he chooses to show us reveals
a hidden truth about reality (Rosenkranz 7, 9).

There are actually a number of issues here, not least among them
involves trying to identify the student's thesis. One problem is
that the first-person comments are too weak to be thesis ideas.
Next problem: if the student writer thinks her central idea is her
final sentence in the passage above (conventional placement), her
difficulty is that she has cited a source for that claim and, therefore, it *cannot be her thesis* idea.

Source boundaries are particularly problematic here as well.
The writer shifts from first to third person, and so the reader
clearly identifies her ideas when she is using first person, but
when she shifts to third person it becomes unclear. Her citation
indicates two pages, implying a good amount of material comes
from Rosenkranz. So, is everything written in third person to be
attributed to Rosenkranz? I do not know until I question the
student. I may, in fact, be incorrectly attributing her ideas to
Rosenkranz. A possibility for a thesis comes in the following statement: "With ceaseless curiosity and sensitivity, Freed approaches
the tragedies and summits of life, zealous to document the unexpected, the unforeseen, presenting the viewer with unsought aspects of pain and joy." Is this authored by my student writer (in
third person), or does the idea belong to the critic Rosenkranz? I
am also concerned because of the sophisticated diction of the
statement: is some or all of this Rosenkranz's language (source of
language plagiarism)? Again, even if she is citing the source of
information, she is not indicating that the language is not her
own. I will have to do two things: get a copy of Rosenkranz's

criticism and interview the student. I may be wrong. This student may be a sophisticated writer. I will need to check.

A way to correct the source boundary difficulty here would be to separate out the voice shifts. First person in one paragraph (with some additional elaboration of ideas) and third person in the next (for the properly summarized or paraphrased source material from Rosenkranz). Another option the student has is to introduce the critic's name into the sentence construction to create a boundary (*wherever it is appropriate to do so*). Here is one conjectured example: "Although [Freed] is a reporter, [Rosenkranz maintains that] his focus is not sensationalist" (7, 9). If the student is incorporating some exact language from Rosenkranz, she will need to enclose partial quotes within quotation marks.

Varying the methods of source documentation is one issue, though, and boundaries are another. A student needs to be savvy and aware of a need for boundaries so that the reader of the essay is not wrongly attributing all of the ideas to the critics when some of them (hopefully, most of them) come from the student. A very basic beginning phrase, such as "According to Showalter," or a slightly more sophisticated statement that tries to achieve synthesis—"Showalter elaborates on this point when she . . ." would suffice (along with precise location of the idea(s) in Showalter's essay)—would achieve variety in the presentation of source documentation and even more significantly would create boundaries between the writer of the research paper and the external voices of the sources integrated.

I also advise students to separate summary out of their own paragraphs of analysis (written in response to the summarized material). They can then cluster source information as separate from their own, creating a boundary through essay structure, through paragraphing. Obviously, summary paragraphs will conclude with a parenthetical source tag.

There are many handbooks that cover proper source integration, most notably the *MLA Handbook for Writers of Research Papers*, and these make excellent desktop references.

Tools for Identifying Plagiarism

> ### Recommendations
>
> 1. Keep student portfolios to have access to authentic writing samples
>
> 2. Become a discerning reader—recognize voice shifts from student to expert
>
> 3. Check suspicious passages using an electronic search engine
>
> 4. Consider using a subscription service (such as Turnitin) to check student papers against electronic sources
>
> 5. Check for print-based plagiarism (school and local libraries)
>
> 6. Vary topics assigned to avoid the passing down of papers through the years
>
> 7. Do not avoid confrontation: conference with students you suspect of plagiarism—they should be able to explain how they arrived at their interpretations

The First Tool

Clearly, teachers must have in-class writing samples as a basis of comparison early on, well before the first take-home essay is assigned. Several examples of students' writing should be kept on file, in case documenting of plagiarism becomes necessary later in the year. These portfolios must include both literary analysis writing and personal writing. The assignment of in-class writing will allow you to gauge writing style, authenticity of voice, and critical thinking ability before you are confronted with a non sequitur in a student's take-home essay.

Filing in-class writing samples in a portfolio enables you to keep track of each student writer's evolution, progress, during the course of the school year. I allow my students to use their texts when writing in-class essays because I want academic arguments that are grounded in evidence and are not mere opinion, reflecting the balancing act that is academic writing. Primary source quotes included must be fully responded to, justifying their inclusion. In these essays, you will see the authentic attempts of students to come to terms with challenging primary sources. Here is true dialogue—perhaps unpolished, but clearly original.

If you fear students have already read an online source, such as LiteratureClassics, in preparation for an in-class essay, then give them, instead, a short story they have never seen before (from an anthology you distribute to them—do not photocopy a story and run into copyright issues yourself). Have them do a cold literary analysis of the text. In reading their responses, you will be able to evaluate their original writing and critical thinking skills. You can justify this "cold reading" because your English class should have a component that is skills-oriented: you are preparing them to be analytical, insightful readers for the rest of their reading lives. If your instruction is too content-oriented, if you have them memorize facts from novels, plays, and poems, then you are encouraging regurgitation and rote memorization, not very far removed from their own plagiarism modes. You are feeding them and expecting the same material spit back at you—not very pleasant. I want to encourage you to give your students a bone to gnaw on. Then examine the marks they leave on it—much more interesting, perhaps even artistic.

Over the course of the school year, you expect to read stronger critical writing than these initial attempts; however, these samples will serve as models for comparison (sometimes to show protective parents, should that need arise). Essentially, you are documenting style, voice, sensibility, and critical thinking skills. This record is the first tool in your battle against forgery. You will note if they retell or analyze (topically or deeply). This will also help you tailor the class instruction of writing. You can target writing instruction to meet particular weaknesses and needs.

The Second Tool

Become a careful and discerning reader yourself. You can hear the voice of the outsider (the scholar, expert, writer) because you are now familiar with your students' abilities as writers and critical thinkers. A partial quote from an external source (without quotation marks) should jump out at you. A highly sophisticated interpretation should be obvious to you. A particular word choice should stand out against the backdrop of students' typical voice and their competence (or incompetence) with language. Sentence structure should be examined for sophistication; an unusual punctuation choice or a complex sentence should be noted. All of these should be red-flagged to be checked on later. I pencil in a vertical line where there is suspicious material. (If I find later that I am wrong when I check up on the student, then the mark is easily erased.) I am ready to sit down at my computer and check.

The Third Tool

Electronic search engines are most helpful when partial or complete expressions have been lifted by the student and can easily be searched for an exact match online. My supervisor at West Milford High School in New Jersey, Margaret Valentine, shared with me an effective method of verifying material: select a dubious phrase or full sentence, then select a search engine such as Google, AltaVista, Vivisimo, or Internet Essay Exposer (this last one will use several search engines at once), and input the phrase (enclosed within quotation marks) into the search engine. If the student has plagiarized electronically accessible material, you will get an immediate link to the source.

Occasionally, savvier students (those who have been caught before, through use of the above method) will scramble the language of the source from which they have appropriated material, so it will be harder to find an exact match. If you are fortunate, there may be a single expression that they neglected to scramble, and you can use that to call up the source. Again, these singular expressions stand out because they are obvious extractions: they present sophisticated diction or ideas or sentence structure. If you are not so lucky as to happen upon a suspicious expression, then I recommend removing the quotes enclosing what you selected to check—you risk finding an extraordinary number of irrelevant hits, but you can still be successful. You have to make educated guesses about which language to use and which words, if any, to enclose in quotation marks. For example, if students found the classic theme of the doppelganger in "The Fall of the House of Usher" and they recognize that using the precise literary term would be too obvious, they might use the expressions "mirror image," or "double image" instead. I would check this by inputting a phrase such as duality in "The Fall of the House of Usher." I would still want to enclose the story's title in quotes—because, if I do not, I will get many irrelevant links that make use of the common words *house* and *fall*. This search for dual imagery may lead me to the doppelganger information, and I may trace how the idea was used by students in their papers.

Keep in mind that electronic search engines are obviously only searching online sources; if you suspect students have plagiarized and you cannot prove that they have used an online source, you must obviously check hard copy sources.

The Fourth Tool

Another electronic tool is Turnitin (Turnitin.com); your school or district can subscribe to this service. You can also subscribe to it yourself, at your own expense. It offers an assignment inbox that will allow you to keep files of particular assignments and check entire class sections of student papers against online or electronically published sources, while you do your other work—lesson planning, parent phone calls, grading exams. How many of us resent the time taken away from lesson planning when we are forced to track down plagiarized sources for one or two student papers? I have sometimes spent hours checking a single essay.

With Turnitin, you have the option of cutting and pasting a passage of a student's essay. The site will check for matches and report back quickly. Here, again, you are selecting what you think looks suspect. You can also have your students submit papers via Turnitin.com. You can require this type of submission only if all students have equal access to computers: if your school allows students access to computers after school hours, in a media center or computer lab. Then you can check the complete essays of all your class sections: they will be scanned for instances of plagiarism. This is even easier as you are not selecting the suspicious passages. Turnitin checks all papers and determines whether or not any incorporated material was plagiarized from online or electronic sources. Turnitin will calibrate the amount of appropriated material students integrated into their essays through a color range system.

Turnitin uses three databases to check for plagiarism: Internet sources, electronically published works, and student submissions (prior as well as current)—it will check student essays from other schools against the essays of your students.

Remember that although this service utilizes extensive databases of online or electronic materials for correlation, only these sources can be checked—you may need to check hard copy sources on your own. If Turnitin does not validate your suspicion, it does not mean that your suspicion is unfounded.

The Fifth Tool

Print-based plagiarism, plagiarism from hard copy sources, requires more effort to prove. Many of us are skilled at detecting this type of plagiarism, having practiced detection of plagiarism in the pre-electronic ages.

Students are less likely to go down this path, because it requires more energy; it is clearly less convenient. Students most likely to plagiarize often have an aversion to libraries and books in general. However, students realize that it will involve more effort on the part of the teacher to prove this type of plagiarism, and that there are some teachers who will not check essays carefully. Their reputations are already widely established in their schools. Papers have been recycled for years to this teacher, who has yet to recognize this deception. It is likely that this teacher is not thoroughly reading the essays he or she is grading, and students are well aware of this fact.

For those of us who are vigilant, we will enter the library as detectives on the trail of a more intelligent thief. It will be a challenge. What the offender has failed to fully consider is that, as teachers of English, we are in our element in the library, and that finding the appropriated material involves a short trip to the card catalog or electronic catalog of our school library (in unusual situations, we might need to try the town library).

If you do a subject search of the author, you can locate the critical collections and scan them for the ideas and language you believe were appropriated: check the table of contents and the index. Periodical sources—the sources students generally loathe the most because of the two-step process of index search and catalog search involved in accessing articles—can usually be saved for checking as a last resort. Periodical sources that students may have used would most likely have been retrieved online and therefore already checked by Turnitin. If you do not have access to Turnitin, you can check for these sources using online search engines. As strange as it may seem, the student's own bibliography may also give them away, particularly if you are dealing with source of language plagiarism. Do not neglect to check hard copies such as *Monarch Notes* and *CliffsNotes*, which may still be lying around at home from the pre-electronic age. In my school, these study guides are kept in the bookroom for the purpose of checking for print-based plagiarism.

The Sixth Tool

Recycled papers are a problem as well. Essays of older siblings and friends may be turned in as students' own work. Family and friends are often happy to help out students in dire straits, at the eleventh hour. Varying reading assignments from year to year, if you have the flexibility in curriculum to do so, can help thwart this approach to plagiarism. Modifying topics assigned, if you do not have the flexibility to select different texts from year to year, will also help you identify recycled papers, because they will be off topic. You can also vary the length of the writing assignment. I once had a student submit a twenty-five-page paper when I asked for a twelve-page paper—a bit too zealous.

Purchased papers are usually not seen at the high school level; most students would consider this a waste of gas money. (College students, unfortunately, have the opposite view—they see this money as an investment in their education.) I have heard of high school students approaching fellow students and offering to pay a few bucks to have their papers written for them. One can refer to filed writing samples (student portfolios) to compare voices, if necessary.

The Seventh Tool

Confrontation—not exactly conferencing—can also be used. I have talked to students privately, while the others were working on a project in the library, or after school hours, to inquire first about the content of their papers. I have them explain how they arrived at their insights—what evidence from the primary source led them there, when the central (thesis) idea first occurred to them. Do they have their freewriting from the first stage of the process? Can I see it? Can they show me, concretely, in their freewriting, the progression of thoughts leading up to the thesis idea? Can they explain the literary device that they described here? How did they identify it? Did they consult outside sources not documented in the paper? (Notice when I slip in that question.) When was it that the theme of the story emerged—on the last page of the novel, in the middle? What does this rather sophisticated expression here mean? Can they rephrase it in the vernacular?

Then I move to the process itself: how do they paraphrase—what is their particular strategy? Why did they quote here instead of paraphrasing? How hard was it to find the sources used in the paper? Have them talk about the research process. Have them discuss how they organized the paper—why did this point follow that one rather than precede it? Keep it spinning—they may flinch or they may confess.

You will find that you are in a less compromising situation if you have done your homework ahead of time. Refer to Chapter 4, "Strategies for Avoiding Plagiarism."

The Multicultural Context:
En homage

The multicultural context cannot be ignored in any serious discussion of composition. Second language students (international and immigrant students) enter our classrooms, at both the secondary and college levels, with different approaches to composition and research writing. Their writings embody a cultural perspective of composition, which impacts form, style, and content.

In "Embracing a Multicultural Rhetoric," Lisle and Mano offer the following as an instructional approach: "The examination of differences among diverse language groups and rhetorical styles [because it] enables students to understand that correctness is contextual, not absolute" (24). This approach validates diversity of expression.

In the U.S. school system, at all levels of learning, there are standards against which second language students' academic writings will be measured. This is the context of evaluation.

As writing instructors, we must allow for diversity of expression even as we evaluate writing against a Western model of composition. The progression of freewriting into formal composition will enable teachers to integrate, rather than marginalize, other cultural approaches to writing. In their freewriting, students explore a topic in whatever way they wish, including within a cultural context that offers familiarity and security—one that encourages meandering and would allow for a collective voice. Freewriting offers students who are uncomfortable with personal writing an opportunity to try on the subjective voice in an informal writing experience.

In terms of expectations of source integration and documentation, what is considered individual property within a Western cultural setting may be considered collective property in other cultural settings. Therefore, to expect ESL students to document sources without a background in research composition in a Western context is to set up these students for failure. We must provide this background in source documentation and in the subjective framework of research. But for these lessons to be meaningful, we must understand and respect the cultural context of the student writer. We cannot dismiss other approaches to writing; we must value them as alternative ways of understanding and communicating knowledge. Through a progression from freewriting to formal writing (which I have recommended in Chapters 2 and 4 for native speakers) we can move toward recognition and validation of several approaches to composition (with the Western cultural setting as a backdrop, not because it offers a better form of composition, but because it is the educational setting of assessment).

Often, the referencing of sources in other cultural contexts is much more general and informal. Specific referencing may be viewed, in these settings, as unnecessary. The collective body of knowledge of some cultures is shared in such a way that citing the individual author of an idea is superfluous. One is expected to know. Incorporating the ideas of established authorities is in itself acknowledgment, a paying homage to a cultural inheritance of knowledge through the integration of this knowledge into the composition process. What we consider external knowledge has been internalized into a collective body within the culture.

Ilona Leki, in her book *Understanding ESL Writers: A Guide for Teachers*, explains it in this way:

> Views of knowledge or of writing as personal property may exist in cultures close to our own, but attitudes may be quite different in other cultural settings. In some places in the world, students are encouraged to learn/memorize the writings of the learned of antiquity and to use those, not their own thoughts, in their writing. For these students, originality in the sense that we use the terms may seem immodest and presumptuous. (71)

Leki speaks of the difficulties ESL students have in writing personal essays, writing within the framework of the subjective stance.

Lisle and Mano also consider how cultural context impacts the development of the "writer's identity" (14). They maintain that writing against the backdrop of American individualism, with its emphasis on the cultivation of original voice and perspective, creates difficulties for some international and immigrant writers when they are assigned personal essays (14). In extrapolating this, we can see how these students are likely to have difficulty, as well, with an original interpretive position necessary for academic writing.

It is worth mentioning that native speakers, because they have had the dubious book report training imprinted in their composition process, may also struggle with a subjective position in academic writing, though typically they do not have difficulty writing the personal essay: they know it requires the personal acts of expression and reflection. Native speakers do not always know how to apply this subjectivity to topic-oriented writing because—too often—it has not been required of them.

This speaks to what is most troubling, in terms of educational practice, and what I have repeatedly been cautioning against in this book—the emphasis on retelling over researching. Sterling criticizes the incorrect approach to research practiced in many high school classes. He outlines the faulty approach: "the way to write a 'report' is to go to the library, copy from a book . . . put a title page and table of contents on it, make a fancy folder, and receive an A" (Sterling qtd. in Thompson and Williams). In their article "But I Changed Three Words! Plagiarism in the ESL Classroom," Thompson and Williams point out that these secondary school teaching practices, which reward reporting, create even more difficulties for the ESL learner heading off to college, where analysis and not restatement is valued. Their recommendation is that assignments should be developed and classroom conversations should be conducted so that students fully understand "plagiarism as a technical, ethical, and cultural issue" (Thompson and Williams).

Problems overlap for native English speakers and ESL students when they are assigned academic, topic-oriented essays in college, requiring a unique position with respect to the topic. I am not sure where the subjective eye/I got lost in American education: somewhere between the "Special Me" poster the student creates in Pre–K and the student's first college composition course where it has to be reopened (propped open with a toothpick). If we are not teaching students to analyze, but merely restate, we are failing two student populations at once.

Ling Shi's article "Textual Borrowing in Second-Language Writing" considers the role that writing assignments play in the incidence of language and information appropriation. Her study examines both second language (Chinese students, in her study) and native speaker populations. She selected the tasks of summary and opinion writing for her test groups and found that

> the summary task seemed to demand that students select more information or use more words from the source texts than the opinion task. Students who wrote the opinion essays might have avoided using source texts either because they regarded [. . . them] as optional [. . .] or simply because they did not know how to incorporate source information in expressing their own opinions. In comparison, students who wrote the summaries, especially the Chinese students, copied more or less verbatim from source texts. (180–81)

For me, this points again to the overwhelming tendency of teachers to have students report (across the board and across the curriculum) rather than analyze. In most instances, students merely copy with or—even more troubling—without citations, which speaks to questions of authorship and authority. Outside source information embodies the voice of authority, a voice with which even native speakers are reluctant to tamper, so they incorporate language without enclosing exact language within quotes (source of language plagiarism). When providing a citation, students view this as acceptable summary, which it is not.

If we encourage more "opinion" or critical responses, we teach students to have a voice and to claim authorship of ideas. This prepares them to approach the task of summarizing with more confidence. Certainly, we need to teach students how to summarize. It is an important skill, and we need to more explicitly describe the process of summary as digesting material and highlighting main ideas in the student writers' words with the required parenthetical citation tag. But we need to give them confidence first. Clearly, there will always be students who take the easy way out and recopy, but perhaps we can decrease their numbers if we help students establish a voice that can face the authority (the passage to be summarized) eye to eye; perhaps the mirror image approach will be shattered by students' newfound sense of self.

Leslie Croxford, in the essay "Global University Education: Some Cultural Considerations," gives us some additional insight into the cultural context of ownership of ideas:

> In the American university contexts in which I have worked in the Middle East and in Southern Europe, the host culture tends not to vest authority for utterances in the individual. This characteristic does not imply that people do not have personal opinions. They certainly do—a cacophony of them. But that which is to be uttered for serious public attention is expected to come from an authoritative source. The nature of such authority varies in different societies. And, within one society, it might come at different times, as the occasion requires, from a religious or secular source, or even from a member of one's family. (57)

Without an understanding of other cultures, we cannot be quick to condemn second language students for errors in source attribution. We act in ignorance if we act without knowledge of the cultural contexts that serve as settings for the composition process. Some productive strategies that recognize cultural context in the process come from Lisle and Mano, including having students create their own narratives to later analyze within the framework of culture and individual perspective (21–22). In other writing exercises, students navigate, exploring ways of expressing their thoughts and understandings from a cultural perspective against the backdrop of conventional academic discourse (Lisle and Mano 22–23).

As instructors, we cannot take an impenetrable, authoritative approach. Spellmeyer's observations are worthy of consideration, not only in terms of a multicultural context, but, more broadly, in general teaching practice:

> [in] conventional writing instruction [. . .]we set one language sharply at odds with the other—the correct against the incorrect, the high against the low. Obliged to choose, student-writers automatically lose both. Unable to be heard in the words they can

claim as theirs, they learn to speak a language which remains the property of others. (5–6)

If students remain outside their writing, they are disengaged—without a point of entry into subject or into self.

In addition, it becomes harder for these students to discern the boundaries—where their ideas end and those of the outsiders begin. In fact, as Spellmeyer suggests, if they try to satisfy the requirements of instructors without satisfying themselves, they take over a language that is not their own and are unsuccessful in original thinking because conventional writing imposes a false voice and a projected facade of understanding. In this faulty process, the authentic voice is lost. The "common ground" Spellmeyer speaks of can be achieved, as he maintains, "whenever we acknowledge the unfamiliar as a way of reseeing ourselves, our words, our daily lives" (134).

We must share understandings of composition and source incorporation, learning from each other in a more realistic and more productive attempt at teaching meaningful academic writing that will be acceptable in college and university settings. Of course, we must expose students to rhetorical modes and correct source citation because knowledge of these conventions is required in an American academic environment. But we must respect students' cultural approaches to composition, learned through a modeling of ideal form in their own cultural settings.

If we impose rather than invite, we jeopardize the vitality of student writing and end up with dry texts that conform but do little else. To emphasize my point, I have excerpted the following passage from *The God of Small Things* (which, though it is a work of fiction and not academic discourse, evidences the tension between cultural contexts—the language imposed and the rebellion through reinvention). Arundhati Roy (an Indian writer/activist who writes in English) creates a stunning chaos where words bump into each other and English conventions such as rules of capitalization, standard usage, conventional punctuation, and completeness in sentence structure are broken as rhythm and rhyme dominate. Words collide (a visual for foreign worlds colliding, as well) in an exhilarating and refreshing reinvention of English, a defiance that makes her work exquisitely original:

Scurrying hurrying buying selling luggage trundling
    porter paying children shitting people spitting coming
    going begging bargaining reservation-checking.
Echoing stationsounds.
Hawkers selling coffee. Tea.
Gaunt children, blond with malnutrition, selling smutty
    magazines and food they couldn't afford to eat themselves.
Melted chocolates. Cigarette sweets.
Orangedrinks.
Lemondrinks.
CocaColaFantaicecreamrosemilk. (284)

This is an example of fiction, of creative and not expository writing, but there is a lesson embedded in it for me as a writing instructor. We do not want writing, even academic writing, to be lifeless. As a postmodern writer, Roy's writing shares characteristics with other postmodern writers, notably in the fragmentation of narrative. And the writing, of course, shares characteristics with the great modern writer Joyce, who was also rebelling against the language of colonization by destroying and resurrecting a language in new form. In addition, Roy's protagonist is an adult remembering in the voice of the child (like Joyce's perspective in "Araby," for example) and part of what we hear in the writing is the child's voice and a child's love of sound in language and a playfulness and a testing of language against meaning. All of that aside, the writing's energy comes from a tension of cultures in negotiation for territory that gives it vitality and authentic voice.

    Although we are teaching academic writing, we cannot discount the cultural context. It invigorates the writing because it is connected to the writer's identity, informing the writer's voice—and, yes, it can be incorporated into academic writing. Some of this energy can be commuted to the informal writing process and then to the final product (formal writing). This cannot happen if we impose order first—start with the first draft of the formal essay. Freewriting would allow cultural context to serve as the true and comfortable setting in which the second language student could get started on the process of writing a personal essay or a research paper.

    But we must distinguish between process and product. The product will be evaluated against the Western academic backdrop. If we do not prepare students for the academic environment in which they will be evaluated, we are failing them. In fact, we are playing a subtle power game with these students if we are not requiring academic form and correct attribution of sources—because we are making a decision for them, and, therefore, we are not inviting them in to make their own decisions regarding academic success—thus allowing them to accept or to defy Western conventions.

Croxford calls on teachers to commit the "harder act of cultural imagination" (60) to understand where the students are coming from—literally—when they compose thoughts (not always their own) in written form. I believe that through both freewriting (allowing students a cultural mooring for comfortable expression) and conferencing with international and immigrant students (in process, moving toward transitioning to formal writing) we can achieve this in a two-way direction—both student and instructor coming to understandings and expectations regarding the other. We must sanction a voice that is both collective and individual. Croxford leaves us a final consideration: "This is not to say that faculty should require less of their students. Rather, they should demand more of themselves" (60).

In terms of form, linear argument is the underlying template of Western writing. To some extent this is an oversimplification, but it is usually the skeletal form of most academic writing. Perhaps it is better to say that it is most widely taught and encouraged as the underlying form of academic writing. Anecdotal writing embedded in traditional argument would be viewed as digression in a Western cultural context, but the model for writing in many other countries is nonlinear: it is meandering in form and often more narrative in form. It is appropriate for slight anecdotes to be used as illustrations even as these anecdotes seem (in our evaluation) to stray from the topic idea. Ultimately a conclusion is reached, but the path is more like freewriting, more interesting and often more intricate because of the more circuitous routes taken. The American fast-food approach of getting right to the point is often absent in the writing of international student populations where there is a stopping to embellish and expand parameters. It is more like Spellmeyer's description of form coming to being in the process of composition (55). In Western writing, students may be so conscious of academic form requirements that these requirements compress their writing: form, then, is not intrinsic to their composition process but is extrinsic to it. American students pour writing into molds; ESL students create interlocking streams that continually renew the writing landscape (obviously, a less artificial process).

In the essay referenced earlier, "Embracing a Multicultural Rhetoric," Lisle and Mano consider the writing forms of other cultures and recommend that we "counter our ethnocentric biases by learning about as wide a range of rhetorical models as possible" (16). They list some examples (within these categories there is, of course, much diversity) including a more intricate, meandering style, which emerges as a form in the original languages of some Asian cultures; religious underpinnings, as a foundation of form in Arabic writings; sound devices informing rhetorical modes in the writings of African cultures (Asante in Lisle and Mano 18); and narrative forms and story collages in the writings of Native American cultures (Lisle and Mano 16–18).

Esha Niyogi De and Donna Uthus Gregory refine the definition of multiculturalism as inclusive of "class; gender; geographic region; nationality; urban, suburban, or rural affiliation; and major socializing forces like popular culture, politics, and religion" (123). According to De and Gregory, these layers of identity clearly impact a student's centering of himself or herself within an academic environment: "they determine the degree to which a student speaks and writes a language akin to the formal academic or tends to subvert that language and thus needs to be translated into it (and therefore colonized by it)" (123). De and Gregory present teaching strategies that work toward decolonization. Through individual and group experiences they have students draw the inner subjective voice outward, broadening then to cultural context, and lastly to argumentative structure. Rather than imposing the structure of academic discourse on student writers, they work from inside out in the process (129–32). The nature of a "writer's identity," raised by Lisle and Mano, is an interesting consideration here. Some students will have difficulty with the subjective stance required, the personal reaction to the literary text, for example.

Juan C. Guerra, in his essay "The Place of Intercultural Literacy in the Writing Classroom," assists us in understanding the process in which students are superimposing the lenses through which they, as writers, see the world before them. He recommends that we as writing instructors

> challenge the idea that each of us is in only one community at a time, as though discourse communities were so distinct and unchanging that moving among them literally involved crossing a border. Finally we need to encourage our students to see themselves as members of several communities at once instead of as people engaged in a one-way transition from their community to ours. (250)

Envisioning the world collectively and individually offers a range of understanding we are not likely to encounter in the writings of native speakers; by exploring other ways of conceiving and expressing, all students will benefit through cultural exchange. It is through a recognition of identity (cultural and individual) that point of view emerges. And point of view must be cultivated to encourage original ideas and expression. Freewriting, which by its nature is open, readily accommodates point of view.

Conclusion

Writing *en homage,* as we see, is not just practiced by other cultures; even native speakers succumb to the voice of authority (though native speakers will usually cite the source because of previous modeling within a Western context). It will probably be easier to teach American students, who have more experience in the writing of personal essays, to adopt a subjective stance in academic writing. It will be challenging, obviously, to teach students whose cultural context has cultivated a more collective voice in composition to take a subjective position. But, potentially, the most refreshing, less template-sounding writing may come from other cultural contexts. Expressing a collective voice, its resonance preserved, can certainly be realized in freewriting, and with citation it can speak in formal writing as well. For some second language students it will be difficult to take a subjective stance, but perhaps they can be encouraged to experiment with voice in their freewriting. Rather than impose voice, style, and form from the outset, we may ultimately receive work that is more richly textured in final form than we encounter in the formal writings of our native speakers.

Negative Space

In twentieth-century abstract art, the concept of "negative space" is an important one; it is the absence of presence, the space that fills the open sculpture. The positive space is the design, the boundaries delineated by the artist. The artist creates the piece to contain space: space enters and fills the construction. It is in this negotiation of space that I wish to place my analogy. The student writer is the artist creating context through the subjective eye, in response to knowledge: the student writer renders interpretation, defining the space that the others (specialists, scholars) will occupy. The outsiders, whose voices will fill the volume of this framework (the secondary sources), exist as the negative space. I do not mean this in a qualitative way: I mean it in terms of dimension and originality. The subjective eye—the giver of form and design through unique vision—belongs to the student in the research essay, who creates the positive space, what we recognize as substance. The essay is a contribution to knowledge, and it should be uniquely the student's own work. This does not mean that student writers' understandings cannot be encountered elsewhere in other sources, that they are the only people to have come up with this way of seeing the subject matter. However, it is in the honesty of their evaluation that we recognize originality: the student writers' individual way of seeing. The original thesis is the organizing principle that gives the essay form and allows for dimension.

I do not mean that we relegate the scholars to a "negative state"; however, we want to emphasize to students the importance of their understandings and stress that these are valid ideas, even though they are often naive.

As students become more educated, their voice and their vision will become more sophisticated, more worldly, more intelligent. We are training them to think for themselves, fostering critical, engaged thinking. As students pick up knowledge and content along the way in their academic careers, we have given them authority of point of view.

Our culture has become a sponge culture of oversaturation: everything is soaked up indiscriminately. Let us teach our students how to discriminate. Let us teach them that they have the right to discriminate, to reject some scholarly points of view and to embrace others.

We are confronted with what I term "the cult of mediocrity," in this environment of "reality television" and McMansions, amidst the voyeurism of mundane celebrity (an oxymoron?) lives, and the celebration of uniformity. Strangely and somewhat ironically, the "me generation" (out of love of itself?) seeks duplication, a cloning of the individual. But in replicating, this generation lost its original identity, diluted in the average. Individuality self-destructs in endless mirroring: it can no longer see itself in an original state.

WORKS CITED

Barton Fink. Dir. Joel Coen. Prod. Ethan Coen. Perf. John Turturro, John Goodman. Videocassette. Twentieth Century Fox, 1991.

Boyer, Paul, and Stephen Nissenbaum. *Salem Possessed: The Social Origins of Witchcraft*. Cambridge: Harvard UP, 1974.

Capote, Truman. *Other Voices, Other Rooms*. 1948. New York: Vintage, 1994.

Croxford, Leslie. "Global University Education: Some Cultural Considerations." *Higher Education in Europe* 26.1 (2001): 53–60.

De, Esha Niyogi, and Donna Uthus Gregory. "Decolonizing the Classroom: Freshman Composition in a Multicultural Setting." Severino, Guerra, and Butler 118–32.

DeSena, Laura. "Mary Cassatt." *Contemporary Women Artists*. Ed. Laurie Collier Hillstrom and Kevin Hillstrom. Detroit: St. James Press, 1999. 123–24.

Dyson, A. E. "*Vanity Fair*: An Irony against Heroes." Sundell 73–90.

Elbow, Peter. *Writing with Power: Techniques for Mastering the Writing Process*. New York: Oxford UP, 1981.

Gibaldi, Joseph. *MLA Handbook for Writers of Research Papers*. 6th ed. New York: MLA of America, 2003.

Goldberg, Natalie. *Writing Down the Bones: Freeing the Writer Within*. Boston: Shambhala, 1986.

Gould, Stephen Jay. "Sex, Drugs, Disasters, and the Extinction of Dinosaurs." *Discover Magazine*, 1984. Rpt. in *The Flamingo's Smile: Reflections in Natural History*. New York: W. W. Norton, 1985. 417–26.

Guerra, Juan C. "The Place of Intercultural Literacy in the Writing Classroom." Severino, Guerra, and Butler 248–60.

Howie, Sam. "Character, Caricature, and the Southern Grotesque." *The Writer's Chronicle* Feb. 2005: 12–19.

Huber, Richard A., and Christopher J. Moore. "A Model for Extending Hands-On Science to Be Inquiry Based." *School Science and Mathematics* 101.1 (2001): 32–41. *Research Library*. ProQuest. New York University Libraries, NY. 24 Jul. 2005 <http://www.proquest.com/>.

Joyce, James. *A Portrait of the Artist as a Young Man*. New York: Viking Press, 1964.

Kettle, Arnold. "*Vanity Fair*." Sundell 13–26.

Leki, Ilona. *Understanding ESL Writers: A Guide for Teachers*. Portsmouth, NH: Boynton/Cook, 1992.

Lisle, Bonnie, and Sandra Mano. "Embracing a Multicultural Rhetoric." Severino, Guerra, and Butler 12–26.

Mallon, Thomas. Afterword. *Stolen Words*. By Thomas Mallon. San Diego: Harcourt, 2001. 239–50.

Moore, Randy. "Writing as a Tool for Learning Biology. " *Bioscience* 44.9 (1994): 613-17. *Research Library*. ProQuest. New York University Libraries, NY. 24 Jul. 2005 <http://www.proquest.com/>

Morrison, Toni. *Beloved*. 1987. Rpt., New York: Plume, 1988.

Olwell, Russell, and Ronald Delph. "Implementing Assessment and Improving Undergraduate Writing: One Department's Experience." *History Teacher* 38.1 (2004): 31 para. 24 Jul. 2005 <http://www.historycooperative.org/journals/ht/38.1/olwell.html>

"Plagiarism Prevention." *Turnitin*. Paradigms. 1998–2004. 27 July 2004 <http://turnitin.com/static/plagiarism.html>.

Poe, Edgar Allan. "The Fall of the House of Usher." *Points of View: An Anthology of Short Stories*. Ed. James Moffett and Kenneth R. McElheny. New York: NAL Penguin, 1966. 255–72.

Quinn, Patrick F. *The French Face of Edgar Poe*. Carbondale: Southern Illinois UP, 1957

Rosenkranz, Stefanie. Introduction. *Leonard Freed: Photographs 1954–1990*. By Leonard Freed. New York: W.W. Norton, 1992. Rpt. of *Photographies 1954–1990, par Leonard Freed*. 1991.

Roy, Arundhati. *The God of Small Things*. 1997. Rpt., New York: HarperPerennial, 1998.

Ryan, Frank L., and Arthur K. Ellis. *Instructional Implications of Inquiry*. Englewood Cliffs, NJ: Prentice-Hall, 1974.

Severino, Carol, Juan C. Guerra, and Johnella E. Butler, eds. *Writing in Multicultural Settings*. New York: MLA, 1997.

Shakespeare, William. *William Shakespeare: Hamlet: Complete, Authoritative Text with Biographical and Historical Contexts, Critical History, and Essays from Five Contemporary Critical Perspectives*. Ed. Susanne L. Wofford. Boston: Bedford Books, 1994.

Shi, Ling. "Textual Borrowing in Second-Language Writing." *Written Communication* 21.2 (2004): 171–200. *Research Library*. ProQuest. New York University Libraries, NY. 27 Jul. 2005 <http://www.proquest.com/>.

Showalter, Elaine. "Representing Ophelia: Women, Madness, and the Responsibilities of Feminist Criticism." *Shakespeare and the Question of Theory*. Ed. Patricia Parker and Geoffrey Hartman. London: Routledge, 1985. Rpt. in "*Hamlet*: A Case Study in Contemporary Criticism." Part Two. *William Shakespeare: Hamlet: Complete, Authoritative Text with Biographical and Historical Contexts, Critical History, and Essays from Five Contemporary Critical Perspectives*. Ed. Susanne L. Wofford. Boston: Bedford Books, 1994. 220–40.

Spellmeyer, Kurt. *Common Ground: Dialogue, Understanding, and the Teaching of Composition*. Englewood Cliffs, NJ: Prentice Hall, 1993.

Staples, Brent. "Black Men and Public Space." *Life Studies: A Thematic Reader*. 3rd ed. Ed. David Cavitch. New York: St. Martin's Press, 1989. 34–37.

Stevens, Mark. "Goya's Third of May, 1808." *Travel and Leisure* (1982). Rpt. in *The Little Brown Reader*. 3rd ed. Ed. Marcia Stubbs and Sylvan Barnet. Boston: Little, Brown, 1983. 451–54.

Sundell, M. G., ed. *Twentieth Century Interpretations of Vanity Fair: A Collection of Critical Essays*. Englewood Cliffs, NJ: Prentice-Hall, 1969.

Thompson, Leonora C., and Portia G. Williams. "But I Changed Three Words! Plagiarism in the ESL Classroom" *Clearing House* 69.1 (1995): 27–29. *Research Library*. ProQuest. New York University Libraries. 27 Jul. 2005 <http://www.proquest.com>.

Tillotson, Kathleen. "*Vanity Fair*." Sundell 40–54.

Valentine, Barbara. "The Legitimate Effort in Research Papers: Student Commitment versus Faculty Expectations." *Journal of Academic Librarianship* 27.2 (2001): 107–15. *Business Source Premier*. EBSCO. New York University Libraries, NY. 24 Jul. 2005 <www. epnet.com/>.

Walliman, Nicholas. *Your Research Project: A Step-by-Step Guide for the First-Time Researcher*. London: Sage, 2001.

Whitman, Glenn. "Teaching Students How to Be Historians: An Oral History Project for the Secondary School Classroom." *History Teacher* 33.4 (2000):469–81. *JSTOR*. 25 Jul. 2005 <http://www. jstor.org/search>.

Williams, Raymond. "New English Drama." *Twentieth Century*, 170, no. 1011 (1961): 169–80. Rpt. in *Modern British Dramatists: A Collection of Critical Essays*. Ed. John Russell Brown. Englewood Cliffs, NJ: Prentice-Hall, 1968. 26–37.